The Writing Triangle: Planning, Revision, and Assessment

A fresh look at your tired writing process

GRAHAM FOSTER

Pembroke Publishers Limited

© 2010 Pembroke Publishers
538 Hood Road
Markham, Ontario, Canada L3R 3K9
www.pembrokepublishers.com

Distributed in the U.S. by Stenhouse Publishers
480 Congress Street
Portland, ME 04101
www.stenhouse.com

The author gratefully acknowledges students who allowed their work to be included in this book. Thanks also to the following educators for their assistance and advice: Brandon Bailey, Arlene Christie, Elizabeth Cressman, Tracey Miller, Anne Payne, Lisa Squance, and Janeen Werner-King.

We acknowledge the financial support of the Government of Canada through the Book Publishing Industry Development Program (BPIDP) for our publishing activities.

We acknowledge the assistance of the Government of Ontario through the Ontario Media Development Corporation's Ontario Book Initiative.

Library and Archives Canada Cataloguing in Publication

Foster, Graham
   The writing triangle : planning, revision, and assessment, a fresh look
at your tired writing process / Graham Foster.

Includes index.
ISBN 978-1-55138-259-3

   1. English language—Writing—Study and teaching (Elementary). 2. English language—Writing—Study and teaching (Middle school). 3. English language—Composition and exercises—Study and teaching (Elementary). 4. English language—Composition and exercises—Study and teaching (Middle school).
I. Title.

LB1576.F6967 2010   372.62'3044   C2010-903832-0

Editor: Jane McNulty
Cover Design: John Zehethofer
Typesetting: Jay Tee Graphics Ltd.

Printed and bound in Canada
9 8 7 6 5 4 3 2 1

FSC
Mixed Sources
Product group from well-managed
forests and other controlled sources
Cert no. SW-COC-002358
www.fsc.org
© 1996 Forest Stewardship Council

Contents

1 The Writing Triangle in All Writing Tasks

Moving Beyond a Generic Writing Process

To what extent has generic (or general) advice about the process of writing helped you to improve your writing? Many students would answer that generic advice about the writing process can be helpful. However, this advice is often too general to apply to an actual writing task on which a student is working. Students say they need *more specific* planning, revision, and self-assessment strategies.

Writing process guidebooks typically describe the following five stages of composing material:

- Planning
- Drafting
- Revising
- Editing
- Publishing

These guidebooks suggest strategies for each stage of composition. Researchers who study the writing process have discovered that writers who identify and apply strategies for planning, drafting, and revising tend to write better compositions than those who do not employ strategies. However, you need to apply different strategies to succeed when composing different writing forms. For example, you plan and revise a description quite differently from how you plan and revise a story. While generic advice might be helpful to a writer, it is never sufficient in itself.

It is true that some generic strategies apply to all writing forms. However, students say that often these strategies are simply too broad to be useful. This book seeks to help writers overcome this problem. It introduces an approach to writing known as "the writing triangle." Just as a triangle has three sides, this approach to writing features three aspects—specific planning, revision, and assessment strategies—that students can use when creating the following writing forms:

- Description
- Narration
- Lyric poetry
- Exposition
- Persuasion/deliberative inquiry research (paragraphs and essays)
- Business letters
- Formal e-mail messages
- Reviews of television and movie dramas
- Exploratory writing

A section at the back of this book titled "Useful References" gives you detailed information about additional helpful techniques that apply to one or more of these writing forms.

The writing triangle approach will help you succeed in creating effective compositions because the strategies give you focused planning tools and revision criteria. The writing triangle can also guide you in terms of specific assessment feedback as you set personal goals to improve your writing in different forms.

Use the new strategies in this book to re-energize your writing process. At the same time, keep in mind that the generic planning, drafting, revision, and assessment strategies presented in this chapter will also sometimes apply to and help facilitate your writing tasks. Keep these generic strategies in mind and use them as you see fit. Then move on to the specific planning, revision, and assessment strategies that apply to a particular writing form. In addition, turn to the "Useful References" section at the back of this book when you require further information about the following:

- Word Choice
- Conventions
- Sentence Variety
- Transitions
- Organizational Patterns
- Comparisons: From Clichés to Originality
- Titles: Straightforward to Snappy

Besides adopting this double approach to planning, revision, and assessment, consider keeping a Personal Writing Goals Chart. A writing goals chart includes dated notations about what you need to improve and what you have already improved in your writing. This chart will help you to be efficient as you plan, revise, and assess your writing and as you confer about your writing with teachers and others. See the sample below, which shows the beginnings of a personal writing goals chart. (Note that a full-sized reproducible version of this chart appears in the "Reproducible Pages" section at the back of this book.)

My Personal Writing Goals

Goals Identified	Goals Achieved
- Make my words more precise (Sept. 20) - Correct run-on sentences (Oct. 4)	- Revised "Creak-Bang-Thud" to make words more precise (Oct.4) - Revised "The Mirror of Vanity" to correct run-on sentences (Oct. 15)

Generic Planning, Drafting, Revision, and Assessment Strategies

The rest of this chapter describes some practical generic strategies that you can apply as you plan, draft, revise, and assess all forms of writing, both print and on-line.

Brainstorming as a Generic Planning Strategy

Brainstorming is a common and familiar planning technique for all writing forms. You have probably brainstormed with classmates many times to help you plan a piece of writing. Begin by reviewing your writing task.

For example, your task might be to defend a personal judgment concerning the question, "Should the voting age be lowered to 16?" With classmates, you could brainstorm arguments in favor of this action as well as arguments opposed to this action. You could also brainstorm ways to complete the writing task.

As everyone offers ideas, feel free to suggest combinations of ideas suggested by others as well as alternative possibilities. A scribe, often the teacher, notes the ideas on the chalkboard, on chart paper, or on a Smartboard™ as students share them.

Brainstorming might include an activity in which you work with classmates to identify the ideas that have the greatest potential for your writing. The sections on planning in each chapter of this book will help you extend brainstorming to more refined and useful planning strategies. For most writing tasks, brainstorming alone is inadequate as a writing planning strategy.

An important rule in brainstorming is to never criticize anyone's suggestions. Instead, take risks and encourage brainstorming partners to take risks as well as you share ideas in your group.

Using RAFTS as a Generic Planning Strategy

Using RAFTS variables is a helpful generic strategy to use when planning a writing task. You may recall that RAFTS is an acronym (short form) for critical writing variables. RAFTS stands for **r**ole, **a**udience, **f**ormat, **t**opic, and **s**trong purpose.

Sometimes your teacher will give you exact RAFTS variables when assigning a writing task. Make sure you understand these variables as you plan your writing. At other times, your teacher may ask students to decide for themselves the writing variables for a particular writing task. Remember that if your teacher has not assigned a variable or variables, you have some flexibility and can make your own thoughtful choices to suit your piece of writing.

RAFTS Variables

R	Role:	From whose point of view am I writing? My own? Someone else's?
A	Audience:	To whom or for whom am I writing? What is my relationship with my audience?
F	Format:	What type of writing am I completing: a story, an editorial, a persuasive essay, a poem, a blog (and so on)?
T	Topic:	What am I writing about?
S	Strong Purpose:	Why am I writing? What am I trying to achieve in my writing?

Advantages of Using RAFTS as a Planning Tool

Using RAFTS offers several advantages as you plan your writing. First, it helps you focus on your writing task by thinking about which variables are required and which variables are optional. Moreover, RAFTS will help you form ideas for your writing. For example, you might employ different details and arguments if you are writing for an adult audience compared to classmates to persuade them that the voting age should be lowered to 16. Thinking carefully about the audience variable as you plan your writing will help you to select the most appropriate details and arguments. Keeping your audience in mind will make your writing strong.

Generic Drafting Strategies

As you begin work on your first draft of a piece of writing, your goal is to maintain your flow in order to get your ideas on paper. Writer's block can challenge writers at the drafting stage. No matter what the writing task, you can use some of the following strategies to help you deal with writer's block, and thus maintain your flow as you create your first draft.

Beating Writer's Block

1. If you experience writer's block when writing a first draft, you might need to spend more time doing some pre-writing. You can try out a different pre-writing strategy–one that is more appropriate for your writing form. For example, suppose you are drafting an expository essay about effects of human activities on an ecosystem in your area. As a pre-writing strategy, you could organize your main ideas in a flowchart or a concept map.

2. Tell someone what you are trying to write and have a discussion about your purpose in writing. Encourage them to ask questions that will help you clarify your writing goal. Answering questions might give you some ideas about an effective way to begin your writing. Answering questions might also help you to picture in your mind how your writing might flow.

3. Maintain your drafting flow and don't get bogged down trying to write perfect, polished prose. Leave blanks if you can't think of a word. Write "s" above words that may be mis-spelled and check the spelling later.

4. Write on every second line to make your revisions easier. If you are inputting your work on a computer, be careful to save your drafts.

5. When you are drafting text forms such as research reports, explanations, or persuasive writing, you may find it easier to write your opening paragraph *after* you have written the body of your composition.

Note: The generic drafting strategies discussed above apply to *all* forms of writing. Therefore, drafting strategies will not be discussed further in the remaining chapters of this book.

Generic Revision Strategies

No matter what the writing form or task, checking your writing for specific features will prompt you to make helpful additions, deletions, and changes to your composition. Revision criteria take the form of checkpoints such as varied sentences, clear expression, and effective transitions. Researchers who have studied the writing process have confirmed the value of revision according to specific and appropriate criteria.

Applying specific criteria when you revise a piece of writing will help you improve your composition. You will not only improve your revision, however. You will also demonstrate greater competence in applying these criteria when you draft your next composition.

Each chapter of this book highlights revision criteria that are especially important to specific writing forms. Some criteria, on the other hand, are more generic. In other words, these criteria apply to many if not all writing forms.

The criteria listed in the chart on the next page fall into the generic category. On your own or with a partner, check to see if your writing meets these criteria. The "Useful References" section at the back of this book gives some additional information about how to apply these criteria.

A Note About Grammar/Usage

The final question in the grammar/usage section in the chart on page 10 requires some explanation. Have you noticed that rubrics used to assess writing tend to be quite general in their attention to grammar/usage? The reason for this is that the grammar/usage category includes far too many specific items to include in one rubric. Your teacher can recommend reference books that will show you models of standard English usage that can help you in your writing.

Also, your revision partners and your teacher will help you to identify and deal with your own priorities in grammar/usage. The chart on page 11 lists items that often challenge many students.

Since grammar/usage challenges are so numerous, it is wise to focus on your own personal challenges when you revise your writing. If you are prone to errors with run-on sentences or other matters of usage, include matters of usage on your Personal Writing Goals Chart. Refer to a writing handbook to learn about conventional usage. Following your teacher's advice, complete exercises in the handbook to consolidate your learning. Re-write sentences from your own writing to correct your errors. Finally, focus on personal usage challenges when you revise your writing. (See the final point in the Generic Revision Criteria chart on page 10.)

Generic Revision Criteria

Content	Questions to Ask Yourself
• My writing is clear and understandable. • I have included adequate details. • Details that I include relate to my topic.	• Is anything unclear in my writing? • Where do I need to add details? • Do I need to delete details that are unrelated to my topic?
Organization	
• My writing follows a logical order. • I use transitions effectively in my writing.	• What can I do to make it easier for my reader to follow my text? • Where do I need to improve my use of transitions so that my reader can connect the ideas in my text?
Sentence Structure	
• My sentences are complete. • My sentences are varied in construction.	• Do I need to correct any sentence fragments? (Sentence fragments are partial or incomplete groups of words that do not express a complete thought.) • Have I varied the length and the beginnings of my sentences?
Vocabulary	
• My word choice is precise. • My word choice is appropriate for my audience.	• Which words do I need to change so that my meaning is clear for my reader? • Am I too formal or too informal in my choice of words?
Voice	
• I have included interesting and original details in my writing.	• How can I add originality to my details, words, and comparisons?
Grammar/Usage	
• My spelling is correct. • My capitalization and punctuation are correct. • My grammar/usage is conventional.	• Which words do I need to check for correct spelling? • What changes do I need to make so that capitalization and punctuation are correct? • What aspects of grammar/usage do I need to check to ensure clear meaning in my writing?

Usage Chart

Some Commonly Misused Words	Some Commonly Misspelled Words
• affect/effect	• dinning (should be *dining*)
• accept/except	• weird (should be *weird*)
• can/may	• recieve (should be *receive*)
• bad/badly	• preformance (should be *performance*)
• principle/principal	• cafateria (should be *cafeteria*)
• could of (should be *could have*)	• ocassion (should be *occasion*)
• lie/lay	• hieght (should be *height*)
• irregardless (should be *regardless* or *irrespective*)	
• there, their, they're	
• it's/its	

Some Common Capitalization and Punctuation Problems	Some Common Sentence Structure Problems
• lack of capital letters for proper nouns	• sentence fragments
• lack of a capital letter to begin a sentence	• run-on sentences
• lack of capital letters for important words in titles	• wordy sentences
• improper punctuation to end sentences (period/question mark/ exclamation point)	• lack of subject-verb agreement
• improper use of colons and semicolons	• lack of parallel structure
• inconsistent verb tense	• inconsistent verb tense
• unclear pronoun reference	• unclear pronoun reference
• incorrect placement of commas	• misplaced modifiers

Generic Assessment Strategies

Rubrics used in assessing writing typically list expectations for content, organization, vocabulary, voice, sentence structure, and conventions. Rubric scores tell you about your degree of success in completing a writing task. They have an even more important function, however—to help you improve your writing.

Rubrics included in this book have been written in student-friendly language so you can assess your own writing and your classmates'. Just as with the planning and revision strategies in this book, you can use a double approach to assessment. Combine the generic rubric with the specific rubric for the writing form of your composition.

As you use rubrics to assess your own and others' writing, set personal writing goals. Use each rubric to make helpful changes that will improve your writing.

Generic Writing Rubric

	I'm not there yet	I'm getting there	I'm there now
Content	• Readers are not sure about my meaning. • I have included few details related to my topic.	• Most of my writing is understandable. • I could have included additional details in my writing.	• My writing is consistently clear and understandable. • I have included adequate details in my writing.
Organization	• My writing is disorganized. • I use no or few transitions among the sections of my writing.	• My writing is arranged logically, but I could improve the structure. • I use some transitions among the sections of my writing but using more transitions would improve the flow of my writing.	• My writing has a logical structure that makes it easy for readers to follow. • I have included adequate and effective transitions among the sections of my writing.
Vocabulary	• My words are inaccurate, misused, and unclear.	• My words are sometimes appropriate, effective, and purposefully selected.	• My words are consistently appropriate, effective, and purposefully selected.
Voice	• I show little originality in the details I have included. • I show no originality in comparisons.	• I have included a few original details. • I have included one original comparison that is original and effective.	• I have included several striking details that other writers might have overlooked. • I have included more than one original comparison.
Sentence Structure	• I seldom vary the length and structure of my sentences. • I seldom write complete sentences.	• I demonstrate some variety in the length and structure of my sentences. • Most of my sentences are complete.	• I frequently vary the length and structure of my sentences. • All of my sentences are complete.
Conventions	• I make frequent errors in spelling, punctuation, and usage that will confuse my reader.	• I make some errors in spelling, punctuation, and usage.	• I make few errors in spelling, punctuation, and usage.

2 Description

Key Features of Effective Description

This chapter offers strategies and examples that show how writers create powerful descriptions. It offers specific planning, revision, and assessment strategies related to descriptive writing.

Suggest Rather Than Tell

Descriptive writing is most effective when it suggests a strong emotional reaction to a scene or an event. The key word is that good descriptive writing "suggests" rather than tells. For example, you may be disgusted by a messy room. Your description should *suggest* disgust rather than *tell* your reader to be disgusted. You may have felt terrified as you rode in a car that had just blown a tire. Once again, use description to help your reader make an inference about the fear you experienced. In other words, effective description shows rather than tells, and through the showing it conveys your emotional response most effectively.

Activity

Read the following description of a volleyball game. Make an inference about the emotion or emotions suggested by the student writer. Write your inference in your notebook.

> The loud enthusiastic crowd bursts into an uproar, filling the stuffy stale-smelling gym with noise. People on the sidelines bob up and down, up and down, cheering on their players. The home team drills the ball over the net, driving the herd of fans into utter mayhem. Beads of sweat drip down the players' faces, all players twitching and sidestepping. Six hot, perspiring bodies scatter throughout the court ready for anything that is sent their way. They slide to the right and then to the left, quick and swift like a random lightning bolt. The players' look is one of pure concentration and determination like that of a puma ready to pounce. Goose bumps sprout on spectators' arms…. Next point wins. The server strikes the ball over the net. A hush falls over the crowd. Bump, set, spike, the ball is forced downwards, moving at missile speed toward the gym floor. THUD! The ball strikes the solid ground. The gym erupts. Cheering fans and team members dance, hug, and shout! The sweet taste of victory!

Match Sentence Length to Action

When writers wish to suggest speedy action in a description, they can use a series of short sentences. Notice how the following description uses short sentences to suggest rapid play in a baseball game.

> Wood cracks on leather. Cleats dig in. The batter lunges. The shortstop spins. He bobs for the ball. He hurls it to first. The batter's shoe touches. The ball snaps in the glove. Safe!

Planning Strategies for Description

In this section, you will read about some useful strategies to help you plan a piece of descriptive writing. Begin by making decisions about RAFTS variables.

RAFTS Variables

R	**Role**	Decide whether you are a spectator as you describe a scene or event or whether you are a participant in the scene or event. If you are a participant, you will probably write your description in the first person using "I."
A	**Audience**	Since emotional reaction is so important in description, think of the audience with whom you might wish to share that emotional reaction. For example, you might wish to select close friends or family members as your audience.
F	**Format**	Description. Locate a descriptive sentence in a novel or other text form that you are reading. Description often functions as part of a narrative text. Note how the author shows rather than tells about the emotion that is being experienced by someone in the descriptive sentence.
T	**Topic**	Select an event or scene that you feel strongly about.
S	**Strong Purpose**	What emotional response will you strongly suggest through your description: joy, fear, anger, disgust, pity, contempt, sorrow, excitement, frustration, happiness? A strong emotional response to a setting or event will inspire the most powerful descriptive writing.

Firsthand Observation

By capturing and recording details from firsthand observation rather than recollection, you will add richness to your description.

Instead of just imagining a scene or event that you choose to describe, observe it firsthand. With laptop or notebook in hand, jot down details that strongly suggest your emotional reaction to the scene or event. By capturing and recording details from firsthand observation rather than recollection, you will add richness to your description.

When you note observations firsthand, you will probably include details that you may not have expected. The student who wrote the description of the volleyball game jotted details as he observed the game. He then numbered the details to indicate the ones that he thought were most powerful in conveying the emotion (see below).

Activity

Read the numbered list below. It features details mentioned in the student's description of the volleyball game on page 13. Do you agree or disagree with how the student numbered the details from least important (1) to most important (10)? Justify your answer.

Details in Description of Volleyball Game

1. stale smells in gym
3. sweat dripping on players' faces
2. players dart like lightning bolts
4. fans in mayhem when team scores
6. total focus of players
5. six players twitch before they serve
7. hush before final serve for victory
8. bump, set, spike, thud
9. cheering fans, dancing players
10. cheers echo from the gym rafters

Include Sensory Details

Another strategy you can use when planning a powerful written description focuses on including all of the senses: sight, sound, touch, smell, and taste. A pre-writing form like the reduced one shown on page 16 can help you plan your description. You do not need to force the listing of details in every column. However, consider each of the senses as you list details that convey a strong emotional reaction. (Note that a full-sized reproducible version of a pre-writing form for planning a description appears in the "Reproducible Pages" section at the back of this book.)

Techniques for Improving Your Description

Once you have written a first draft of your description, turn to "Useful References" at the back of this book to consider four powerful techniques for improving your description:

- Word Choice
- Transitions
- Organizational Patterns
- Comparisons: From Clichés to Originality

You may wish to include a title for your description. If so, refer to the section called "Titles: Straightforward to Snappy" in "Useful References" at the back of this book.

Pre-Writing Form for Planning a Description

Topic (Scene or Event): _____

Emotional Reaction: _____

Sight	Sound	Touch	Smell	Taste

Specific Revision Criteria for Description

Use color-coded highlighters or sticky notes to identify where your written description contains each of the following characteristics of effective descriptive writing:

- I have included details that strongly suggest my emotional reaction.
- I have organized the details to emphasize the detail that most strongly suggests my emotional reaction.
- I have included colorful words that suggest my emotional response.*
- I included at least one original comparison.*
- I have used a series of short sentences if my description focuses on quick action.

Starred items are characteristics that apply to other writing forms as well as description. In the "Useful References" section at the back of this book, you may wish to check the subsections titled "Word Choice" and "Comparisons: From Clichés to Originality."

Assessment of Descriptive Writing

Use the following rubric to set personal goals to improve your descriptive writing. Remember that you can also apply the criteria listed in the generic rubric in Chapter 1.

Descriptive Writing Rubric

	I'm not there yet	I'm getting there	I'm there now
Content	• Readers are not clear about my emotional reaction because my details do not focus on my emotional reaction.	• My writing suggests an emotional reaction with some details conveying my emotional reaction.	• My writing consistently suggests a strong emotional reaction with all details effectively conveying my emotional reaction.
Organization	• I need to include details that focus on my emotional reaction as the first step to placing the details in an effective order.	• All of the details suggest my emotional reaction. I could have ordered the details more effectively.	• My writing clearly builds to the detail that most effectively conveys my emotional reaction.
Vocabulary	• Few words suggest an emotional reaction.	• Some words effectively suggest an emotional reaction.	• Many words effectively suggest an emotional reaction.
Voice	• I have not included a comparison to help my reader visualize my description.	• I have included at least one comparison to help my reader visualize my description, but it could be more original.	• I have included at least one original comparison to help my reader visualize my description.

3 Narration

Key Features of Effective Narration

Stories require at least one main character (or protagonist) who must deal with at least one problem or conflict. After showing how the conflict affects the main character, you must resolve the story's conflict. Many stories conclude by showing what has changed or what is different for the main character, or how the main character's experiences have affected the life of someone else in the story.

As you read the following story written by a student, review these critical story elements:

- the main character or protagonist
- the conflict
- how the conflict affects the protagonist
- the climax (the resolution of the conflict)
- the ending: what is different or what has changed for the protagonist or for another character in the story

The House on the Hill

It was dark already. Cindy and I had stayed at the library too long. We decided to take the short cut home because if we went the other way, it would be even darker before we got home. We would have to go past the house on the hill but we were not afraid.

We walked quickly for about five minutes. Suddenly, we heard whispering. It came from behind us. Turning around, we expected to see someone, but it was too dark. We hurried on, our hearts beating rapidly. As we walked along a white picket fence, an animal suddenly howled! The sound frightened us.

We could hear whispering again and another howl. I got goose bumps. It sounded too close for comfort. A door creaked in the distance and a man laughed like a hyena. This time we ran! Cindy reminded me of the house that we had passed. I really did not think it was haunted, but I thought so now!

Cindy screamed!

In the moonlight, a tall figure was coming towards us. It did not have a head! It walked kind of jerky. I could not move. All of a sudden my big brother came rushing up on his bike. He zoomed up to the headless man and knocked him down. We were surprised to see Bobby on stilts!

Out of the bushes came Tommy and Joey. They had played a trick on us! I'm glad my brother was worried about me and came to look for me. Now he's going to help us plan a good way to scare those boys back!

Planning Strategies for Narration

In this section, you will read about some useful strategies to help you plan a piece of narrative writing. Begin by making decisions about RAFTS variables.

RAFTS Variables

R	Role	Decide whether you will write in the role of author as storyteller or whether you will write in the first person using "I." You can pretend to be a character in the story if you write in the first person. Remember that many student writers prefer to write in the first person because it reminds them to use personal experiences in their writing.
A	Audience	While you may write a story for a general audience, students often prefer to write for peers or classmates. Think about a story that they would enjoy and learn from.
F	Format	Narrative. Reread your favorite short story, possibly one in a language arts resource or in a collection of short stories. Note the conflict that is central to the story. How is the conflict resolved? How does the ending suggest what has changed or what is different, either for the main character or for other characters in the story?
T	Topic	Without a conflict, you have no story. Your character's conflict is the topic of your story. What problem will your protagonist face? How will the conflict affect the main character? How will the conflict be resolved? How will the conflict change the main character or other characters?
S	Strong Purpose	The most valuable stories are those that help readers understand something about their lives. Writers should not preach themes in a story. Instead, they should *suggest* themes. Endings that show what is different or what has changed for the protagonist or for another character point readers to the story's theme. (Recall that a theme is the key point or message of a story.)

Choosing a Topic (Conflict)

Think about recent conversations you have had with friends. Have you noticed that conversations often turn to problems or challenges that you and your friends are facing?

Story writers recognize that people's conflicts are the stuff of stories. Conflicts can be serious, such as dealing with the death of a loved one, losing a job, worrying about your appearance, or dealing with someone's lies about yourself or someone for whom you care. Conflicts can be lighter in tone as well. Many writers enjoy presenting problems that help them laugh at themselves. Such problems might include losing your bike or your car in the parking lot of a large mall, showing up for a party on the wrong day, or using avoidance strategies when you should be cleaning your room.

Journal Writing as a Planning Strategy

Try journal writing as a helpful planning strategy for your story writing. As you think about conflicts in your own life or in the lives of others, write journal entries about them. Focus on the challenge of dealing with the conflict and the consequences (results) of the choice that someone makes in dealing with the problem. Keep the following questions in mind as you make your journal entries:

- What conflict did you have to deal with?
- Where were you just before the conflict occurred?
- What options did you consider to deal with the conflict?
- What option did you choose to deal with the conflict?
- What was the result of your choice?
- Did you make the best choice?
- How was the conflict resolved?
- Who or what has changed as a result of your dealing with the conflict?

Using a Story Frame to Plan Narrative Writing

Using a story frame as a planning tool helps you to stay focused on your conflict and how to resolve it.

When you are ready to begin more specific planning of your story, consider using a story frame. A story frame prompts you to organize critically important story elements. Student writers can get into trouble in story writing when they include details, often in the form of dialogue, that are unrelated to their story's conflict. Using a story frame as a planning tool helps you to stay focused on your conflict and how to resolve it. Three types of story frames are commonly used: "Planning Frame for Narrative Writing," "Story Bones," and "Story Frame." A blank "Planning Frame for Narrative Writing" appears in the "Reproducible Pages" section at the back of this book. An example of this story frame has been completed on the next page for the story "The House on the Hill" presented earlier in this chapter.

Effective Openings for Stories

As you move from planning your story to drafting your story, decide on an effective opening for your story. The beginning of your story must introduce your main character or protagonist and establish important details of your story's setting—the place and time in which the story takes place. You must also begin the sequence of events that make up your story. Create interest by beginning the story's action as close to the conflict as possible. The following story opening places the protagonist in a specific setting as it quickly points to the story's conflict.

> There I was, helpless, frightened, and stranded. As I glanced around the darkening school ground, I saw them—my attackers. I glanced furtively for my friends. They had vanished. I backed up slowly until I was cornered between the clinking bars and swings. I smiled as they approached but I churned inside.

Endings That Point to Your Story's Theme

Once you have completed the first draft of your story, take a close look at your story's ending. The "Planning Frame for Narrative Writing" (shown full-sized in the "Reproducible Pages" section at the back of this book) prompts you to think about what has changed in your protagonist's life. Sometimes endings focus on how the resolution of the protagonist's conflict has affected someone else in the story. By presenting what has changed for your protagonist or for someone else in the story, you can use your ending to point to your story's theme.

For example, in "The House on the Hill," notice how the ending suggests that we appreciate family members most when we are in trouble. The student writer does not preach the theme. Instead, she uses the story's ending—what has changed for the protagonist—to *suggest* a theme.

Planning Frame for Narrative Writing

TITLE: __The House on the Hill__

MAIN CHARACTER: __A girl ("I")__

SETTING (where/when your story takes place): __Evening; city locations on a walk home__

CONFLICT (the problem your main character must deal with): __Several frightening sights and sounds, especially the headless man coming at the main character and her friend__

CONSEQUENCE OF THE CONFLICT (the effects of the conflict on your main character; show details):

- quick walking

- fast heart rates

- goosebumps

- running

- screaming

- jerky walking

CLIMAX (the resolution of the conflict): __Brother knocks down headless man; girls realize they have been tricked.__

ENDING (an indication of what has changed for the main character or for another character):
__Main character appreciates her brother in a new way and plans to play a trick in return on the boys who tricked her__

Showing Not Telling

Once you have drafted your story, locate a part of your story in which you describe a character's emotion, such as happiness, sadness, fear, anger, relief, nervousness, love, pity, jealousy, or shock. One of the surest ways to improve your story is to show rather than tell about the emotion. The following excerpt shows the terror of two boys who see a bear on their way to their country school.

> First we noticed bear tracks in the snow. In the distance we saw the bear. My heart pounded as I held my breath. I froze where I stood and dropped my lunch pail to the ground. Then we ran.

Use the chart titled "Showing Emotions in a Story" to help you suggest emotion in your story rather than just tell about it. (A blank version of this chart appears in the "Reproducible Pages" section at the back of this book.)

Important Features of Narrative Writing

Word choice and original comparisons are particularly important in narrative writing.

If you need to learn more about the following important features of narrative writing, check the "Useful References" section at the back of this book. You will probably find it easier to include these features in your story writing once you have completed a first draft of your story. Remember that word choice and original comparisons are particularly important in narrative writing.

- Word Choice
- Conventions
- Sentence Variety
- Transitions
- Organizational Patterns
- Comparisons: From Clichés To Originality
- Titles: Straightforward to Snappy

Activity

For "The House on the Hill," suggest one change for each item on the list of features above—especially sentence variety and title. Do you agree or disagree that a different title and additional sentence variety might improve "The House on the Hill"? Justify your answer.

Specific Revision Criteria for Narration

Use color-coded highlighters or sticky notes to identify where your story illustrates selected items from the following list of critical characteristics of narrative writing:

- I have clearly established my protagonist's conflict.
- I have included details to show the effects of the conflict.
- I have checked that dialogue in the story relates directly to the conflict.
- I have included critical details about the time and place of my story.
- My story's climax resolves the conflict.
- The ending of my story shows what is different for the main character or for another character in my story.
- My story suggests a theme—an understanding that may be valuable for my reader.
- My story shows rather than tells about emotion.
- My word choice effectively helps readers visualize events in the story.*
- My story contains at least one original comparison.*
- My story has an imaginative title.*

Starred items are features that apply to other writing forms besides narration. In the "Useful References" section at the back of this book, check the subsections titled "Word Choice," "Comparisons: From Clichés To Originality," and "Titles: Straightforward to Snappy."

Assessment of Narrative Writing

Use this rubric to set personal goals to improve your narrative writing. Remember that you can also apply the criteria listed in the generic rubric in Chapter 1.

Narrative Writing Rubric

	I'm not there yet	I'm getting there	I'm there now
Content—Details	• Readers are not sure about my story's conflict.	• I establish a conflict in my story. Most details relate to the conflict.	• I clearly establish a conflict in my story. Every detail relates to the conflict.
Content—Showing Emotion	• I tell about rather than show emotion in my story.	• I have included one or two details to show emotion in my story.	• I have included three or more relevant details to show emotion in my story.
Organization	• I include inadequate details about the time and place of my story. • I do not resolve my story's conflict and my story's ending needs work.	• I include some details about the time and place of my story. • While I resolve the conflict, my story's ending could more clearly point to a theme.	• I have included critical details about the time and place of my story. • I resolve the conflict of my story and use the ending to point to the story's theme.
Vocabulary	• I need more specific adjectives, adverbs, and verbs to help my reader visualize characters and events in my story.	• While some of my word choices are effective, I could use more specific adjectives, adverbs, and verbs to help the reader visualize characters and events in my story.	• My word choice effectively helps my reader visualize characters and events in my story.
Voice	• I do not include comparisons to help my reader visualize characters and events in my story.	• I include at least one comparison to help my reader visualize characters and events in my story, but the comparison could be more original.	• I include several original comparisons to help my reader visualize characters and events in my story.
Title	• My title does not fit my story.	• My title fits the story but could be more imaginative.	• My story's title is appropriate and imaginative.

4 Lyric Poetry

Key Features of Effective Lyric Poetry

Poems sometimes tell stories and capture dramatic moments. But the most familiar form of poetry focuses on an impression of an event, an experience, a person or a setting. Such poetry is called lyric poetry. Focus on finding poems that you enjoy reading and reflect on how these poems make a strong impression on the reader. By doing so, you will be using strategies that have worked well for other student writers of poetry.

Lyric poetry can be risky because it takes you into a world of vivid experiences and powerful feelings. Sometimes you may not wish to share these feelings and experiences with others. However, poets have discovered that in writing about their impressions of events and experiences, they understand the event and experience better. They understand themselves better, and they help readers understand human experience better as well.

Planning Strategies for Lyric Poetry

In this section, you will read about some useful strategies to help you plan the writing of a lyric poem. Begin by making decisions about RAFTS variables.

RAFTS Variables

R	Role	While you can pretend to be someone else who speaks in a poem, when creating lyric poetry it is best to write in your own role in your own voice.
A	Audience	Plan to write for someone who is interested in you and cares for you. This is important since in poetry you are writing about what truly matters to you.
F	Format	Lyric Poetry. Your reading of lyric poems will improve your writing of lyric poems.
T	Topic	Your subject will be a strong impression of a setting, an experience, a person, or an event.
S	Strong Purpose	Lyric poems help readers understand how poets feel and what they think about a memorable experience.

Your Top 10 Poems

Your reading of favorite poems will help you discover the power of poetry and perhaps the power of your own voice as a poet. You will write poetry more confidently and skillfully when you read widely in poetry and select the poetry that you particularly enjoy.

No doubt you will be studying poetry sometime during your school year. As part of your study, start a list of your top 10 poems—your favorite poems and why you like them.

These poems can be from textbooks, from poetry anthologies, from song lyric collections, or from any other source. Remember that readers enjoy poems for two main reasons:

- Poems capture an emotional experience to which readers can make connections.
- Poems suggest an idea that is important to the reader.

Choosing a Topic for Your Poem

Note that the poems in your Top 10 list probably have strong emotional connections for you. As you select poems that you enjoy, think about something that you could write about in a poem of your own. Focus on an impression—perhaps your favorite place in the world, your most memorable experience, a person who has influenced you, a time of great emotion in your life. This might be a fearful time, a joyous time, a sad time, an exciting time, or a disappointing time.

If you wish, talk to a partner to jog your memory and think about the suggested topics below in any order. Take turns reading and sharing details about

- your favorite place in the world
- your most memorable experience
- a person who has influenced you greatly
- a time of intense emotion in your life

After some discussion with your partner, choose a topic—the subject of your lyric poem. Jot down as many details as possible that you can recall. Focus on images and sensory details that will help a reader experience and understand your topic. (Sensory details appeal to the five senses: sight, hearing, touch, taste, and smell.) In some cases, it will help you to list details if you use firsthand observation of a scene or a picture of a scene.

In applying this strategy to plan a topic for a poem, a student whose father has passed away recalled the powerful feeling that she had when she found his sweater in a chest. When she put on the sweater, she recollected her father's love and realized the importance of capturing her memories of him. The student jotted down the following list of details:

Finding My Dad's Sweater

- Found sweater in packing chest
- Frayed sleeves, faded blue color
- Tried on sweater
- Thought of father's hugs and times when father wore sweater
- Kept sweater on all evening; didn't answer phone calls
- Spent evening sitting and thinking about father

The student focused on details related to finding the sweater and what happened when she found it. Depending on your topic, it might help you to organize a list of sensory details related to sights, sounds, smells, textures, and tastes.

Drafting Your Poem

Now write a draft of your poem. Don't worry about making parts of it rhyme. In fact, rhyme may be unnecessary in your poem. Focus on getting your ideas down on paper. The student drafted the following poem based on the list of details she had prepared. (A revised version of this poem appears below.)

Finding My Dad's Sweater

A frayed sweater in an old chest—
My dad's old sweater!
I put it on and remembered him—
Especially the hugs.
I had other things to do
But I couldn't take off the sweater.

Meaning and Techniques in Poetry

The key concept to keep in mind is that techniques convey meaning in poetry.

As you read poems written by other authors, including poems in anthologies and poems studied in class, you will learn about techniques that poets use so that their poems have a powerful effect on readers. Students often complain that learning about these techniques is boring. It doesn't have to be boring, however, if you relate a specific technique, such as patterns of imagery, to the poem's meaning—the experience, emotion, or themes that the poem conveys.

Notice that meaning is listed at the top of the chart on page 27. The key concept to keep in mind is that techniques convey meaning in poetry.

As you read poems and learn about how poets employ techniques to express meaning in their poems, revisit your own poem. Review each technique, such as effective word connotations, and revise your poem so that it reflects each technique. Would your poem benefit from revisions to your word choice? You will probably make several revisions to your poem as you follow the revision process.

The chart on the next page presents a model that can help you read poems with greater understanding and enjoyment. It will also help you make beneficial revisions to your own poems as you write them.

Revising Poems Effectively

After she had read a number of lyric poems, the student writer completed revisions of her own poem. Note the beneficial revisions compared to the earlier version, especially in terms of use of concise language and original comparisons.

My Father's Old Sweater

I wore his sweater for hours last night
Not to combat the Autumn chill
But imagining again that arms of love
Were round about me and with me still.

The "Useful References" section at the back of this book can help you learn more about critical features of lyric poetry. "Word Choice" and "Comparisons: From Clichés to Orginality" are especially helpful.

Meaning and Techniques in Poetry

Meaning—Theme/Emotions/Experiences	
↑	
TECHNIQUES EMPLOYED TO CONVEY MEANING	
Reading	**Writing**
CONCISE LANGUAGE • Note how poems use concise language to convey meaning	• Where could you be more concise in your poem? What words could you delete?
IMAGERY • Note how effective poems include original word pictures or images. These include literal images as well as figurative images such as metaphors and similes. Literal images are direct descriptions such as "the red barn." Figurative images such as "a barn redder than a fire truck" include metaphors, similes, and other figures of speech.	• Where could you add original literal and figurative images? Have you included clichés that require revision? If so, how could you remove these clichés from your writing?
WORD CHOICE • Poems include words that convey feelings as well as ideas. The suggested meaning of a word rather than its literal meaning is called "word connotation."	• What words could you change or add so that your word connotations are more effective?
STRUCTURE • Poets carefully organize details in a poem. Often poems build to a final key point or a surprising twist at the end.	• Would a change of organization benefit your poem? How can you make your final chunk of text more effective? Would a surprising twist at the end be effective?
RHYME AND SOUND PATTERNS • Poets sometimes use rhyming words to chunk parts of their poem. Also, they sometimes use sound patterns such as imitative harmony (called *onomatopoeia*) to capture the sound of an experience. For example, in the following sentence, "thud" is a word that imitates a sound: "The book fell with a thud."	• Will your poem benefit from rhyme to chunk ideas or are you wiser to write in free verse? Will sound patterns such as imitative harmony be helpful?

Specific Revision Criteria for Lyric Poetry

Use color-coded highlighters or sticky notes to identify where your lyric poem illustrates selected items from the following list of critical characteristics:

- My lyric poem expresses a strong emotional experience and/or suggests a theme.
- My lyric poem uses concise language to convey meaning.
- My word connotations are effective.*
- My lyric poem includes original literal and figurative images.*
- My poem builds to a final key point or surprising twist.
- My poem uses rhyming words to chunk ideas; or my poem does not include rhyming words since they are not helpful in the poem.
- If appropriate, my poem uses sound patterns such as imitative harmony to convey meaning.
- My poem's title imaginatively presents the subject of my poem.

Starred items are features that apply to other writing forms besides lyric poetry. In the "Useful References" section at the back of this book, check the subsections titled "Word Choice" and "Comparisons: From Clichés to Originality."

Assessment of Lyric Poetry

Use this rubric to set personal goals to improve your writing of lyric poetry. Remember that you may also apply the criteria listed in the generic rubric in Chapter 1.

Lyric Poetry Rubric

	I'm not there yet	I'm getting there	I'm there now
Content	• The reader is not sure about my meaning—the emotional experience and/or theme I am suggesting. • I include little or no imagery (word pictures) in my poem.	• While my lyric poem suggests meaning (an emotional experience and/or theme), I could make these more clear. • My poem's imagery could be more original.	• My lyric poem clearly suggests an emotional experience and/or theme. • My lyric poem presents original and effective imagery.
Organization	• The ordering of details in my poem is not effective; I do not build to a key final point or a surprising twist.	• I could improve the ordering of details and end my poem more effectively.	• My poem effectively builds to a key final point or a surprising twist.
Vocabulary	• Few words in my poem suggest an emotional reaction. • My poem needs to be more concise.	• Some words in my poem suggest an emotional reaction but I could have chosen words with more appropriate connotations. • In some parts of my poem, I could be more concise.	• I have included words that effectively suggest an emotional reaction. • My poem is written concisely.
Title	• My title is not clearly connected to my poem's subject.	• While my title is related to my poem's subject, it could be more imaginative.	• My title is imaginatively related to my poem's subject.

5 Exposition

No matter how serious or light-hearted your purpose, expository writing focuses on explanation rather than argument.

Key Features of Effective Exposition

Expository writing seeks to explain or to inform readers about a topic. When your purpose is to explain, your writing needs to be clear, well organized, and complete. Expository writing may serve wide-ranging purposes from serious to lighthearted.

Planning Strategies for Exposition (Paragraphs and Essays)

In this section, you will read about some useful strategies to help you plan a piece of expository writing. Begin by making decisions about RAFTS variables.

RAFTS Variables

R	Role	In expository writing, you are in the role of an expert, that is, someone who is in a position to explain something to others.
A	Audience	Sometimes you have a specific, targeted audience: that is, someone or a group who can apply the explanation. Often your explanation will be offered to a general audience.
F	Format	Expository paragraph or essay. Examples of expository writing that are most familiar to you appear in textbooks in which the writer explains something to the reader. You can find examples of expository writing in many science, social studies, and math textbooks, both in print resources and online.
T	Topic	What is the subject that you are explaining to your readers? What are important points related to your topic?
S	Strong Purpose	While your purpose is to explain, sometimes you will recommend an action related to your explanation. You should think about a possible action to recommend to your readers, either seriously or playfully.

Review Your Purpose in Writing

Your first step in planning expository writing is to review the purpose for your explanation. What do you want your reader to understand? Then brainstorm and list some information related to your purpose.

> **Examples of Purposes for Expository Writing**
>
> - to explain the advantages of living in your community
> - to explain strategies for finding a part-time job
> - to explain positive features of your school
> - to explain challenges facing your city council

By listing information, you can determine whether you need to conduct research on your topic. Sometimes you will need to learn more about a topic before you offer a written explanation.

Use a Planning Form

In expository writing, a topic sentence expresses your purpose. However, note that an effective topic sentence should *suggest*, not state the purpose.

Your second step is to use a planning form for an expository paragraph or essay, depending on how lengthy your explanation will be. If you are writing a paragraph, note the importance of your paragraph's topic sentence, which is often the first sentence. A topic sentence expresses your main idea. In expository writing, a topic sentence expresses your purpose. However, note that an effective topic sentence should *suggest*, not state the purpose. Avoid boring constructions such as: "The purpose of this paragraph is to explain advantages of student tours to the Science World Museum."

Examine the following chart to note how the topic sentences effectively express the purpose and the main idea of an expository paragraph.

Examples of Purposes and Topic Sentences in Expository Paragraphs

Purposes	Topic Sentences
• To explain the advantages of living in your community	• Living in Pleasantville will add quality to your life.
• To explain strategies for finding a part-time job	• Be thoughtful and thorough in your part-time job search.
• To explain positive features of your school	• Students enjoy several advantages at Parkvale School.
• To explain challenges facing your city council	• Belleville City Council must deal with several critical challenges.

A student used the following Expository Paragraph Planning Form to explain some benefits of school tours to the Science World Museum in her community. (Note that a blank version of this planning form appears in the "Reproducible Pages" section at the back of this book.)

Expository Paragraph Planning Form

Purpose: To encourage school tours of the Science World Museum

Topic sentence: Students can benefit greatly from the opportunity to take a school tour of the Science World Museum

Information I could use in my paragraph with the most important point starred:

- Students speak to a guest scientist on each school tour.
- Even students who are not confident in science enjoy playing science games and can learn from hands-on activities.
- Students participate in a "behind-the-scenes" tour not available to the general public.
- For many students, the highlight of the tour is examining forensic evidence to solve a murder case.*

Concluding sentence: Students who think that science is dull will discover how interesting science can be!

From Planning to Drafting

After considering the most effective order of the points listed in the planning form, the student wrote the following paragraph:

Students should not miss the opportunity to take a school tour of the Science World Museum. Even students who are not confident in science enjoy the science games and the hands-on activities. Students speak to a guest scientist on every school tour. In addition, students participate in a "behind-the-scenes" tour not available to the public. For many students, the highlight of the tour involves examining forensic evidence to solve a murder. On school tours at the Science World Museum, students who think that science is dull will discover how interesting and enjoyable science can be.

Writing an Expository Essay

If your explanation requires an essay rather than a paragraph, your success depends on your ability to generate subtopics related to your central topic. For example, if you are explaining the advantages of living in your community, your subtopics might include your community's employment opportunities, social and cultural events, and educational institutions.

For an expository essay assignment, a student chose to compare important features of modern life with how humans might function in the future. The student used the concept map below—an expository essay planning form. Note that a blank version of this planning form appears in the "Reproducible Pages" section at the back of this book. Follow these steps to fill in the form:

1. In the box in the centre, note the topic.
2. In the smaller boxes, identify subtopics. Sometimes brainstorming will help to identify subtopics. Often writers need to do some research to identify subtopics.
3. In the circles, place specific information related to the subtopics. Add subtopic boxes and circles if you have more to write about the topic.
4. Plan an effective introduction and conclusion for your expository essay.

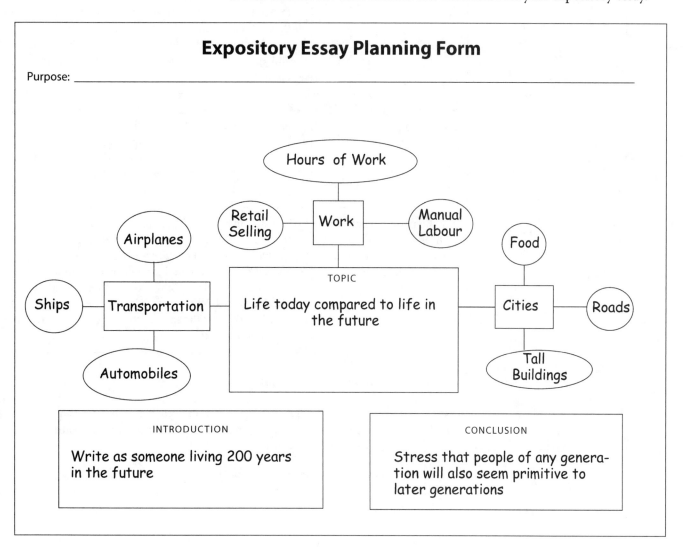

Expository Essay Planning Form

Purpose: _____

Hours of Work

Retail Selling — Work — Manual Labour

Airplanes

Food

Ships — Transportation

TOPIC
Life today compared to life in the future

Cities — Roads

Automobiles

Tall Buildings

INTRODUCTION
Write as someone living 200 years in the future

CONCLUSION
Stress that people of any generation will also seem primitive to later generations

How to Generate Interest in an Introduction

The following chart lists techniques a writer can use to generate interest in the introduction to an expository essay.

Techniques for Creating Interest in an Introduction to an Expository Essay

Technique	Example
• Posing an important question related to your purpose	• Can you imagine losing your life following an accident because the hospital lacked the blood you required for a transfusion? Besides saving the lives of patients in life-threatening situations, blood donors benefit their own health and demonstrate the importance of giving to others in the community.
• Telling a brief anecdote related to your purpose	• An ambulance screeches down Main Street towards the Central Hospital. The attendant radios the hospital that an accident victim who is on her way to the hospital will require a blood transfusion. People should regularly donate blood to save lives. In addition, blood donors benefit their own health and know the satisfaction of giving back to their communities.
• Stating a startling fact or example related to your purpose	• Last year 15,000 Calgarians received life-saving blood transfusions. Without this thoughtful gift from blood donors, these Calgarians may have perished. Besides saving lives, blood donors benefit their own health and know the satisfaction of giving back to their communities.
• Telling about what you think is a foolish or incorrect view related to your purpose	• Many people believe that they do not have to donate blood. Their neighbors can donate the blood required for transfusions. What a short-sighted outlook! Such a viewpoint costs lives. Besides helping others in life-threatening circumstances, blood donors benefit their own health and know the satisfaction of giving back to their communities.

Composing a Powerful Conclusion

Your explanation will have a greater impact on readers if you compose a powerful conclusion. Writers frequently employ the following techniques to create powerful conclusions in expository essays:

- Answer questions posed in the introduction.
- Present a powerful final point.
- Warn the reader.
- Offer a prediction.
- Suggest specific action.

Decide on a Thesis Statement

After you have used a thought web to do some planning, decide on the thesis statement you will include in your introduction. A thesis statement has two goals:

- to express the purpose of your explanation
- to offer a preview of the subtopics that you will develop in your essay

The following chart shows how thesis statements convey your purpose and a preview of your essay's subtopics.

Topic	Thesis Statement
• Advantages of living in your community	• With its employment opportunities, recreational facilities, and educational programs, Pleasantville will add quality to your life.
• Strategies for finding a job	• Thoughtful job hunters prepare lists of job possibilities and leads, research promising companies, and prepare effective resumés.
• Positive features of your school	• For qualified teachers who care about students, an amazing extracurricular program, and an interesting mix of students, register at Parkvale School.
• Challenges facing your city council	• Planning new parks, coping with increased transportation costs, and developing new districts are a few of the current critical challenges facing Belleville.

In summary, an effective introduction in an expository essay captures a reader's attention, presents a thesis statement that makes your purpose clear, and offers a preview of your essay's subtopics. Paragraphs in the essay develop specific subtopics related to the thesis statement. The essay's conclusion should be definite and powerful.

Activity

Following the planning process described above, the student mentioned previously drafted an essay that compared important features of modern life with how humans might live in the future. As you read the final draft of the student's essay, identify the following:

- the thesis statement
- how the student generated interest by means of an effective introduction
- how the student generated interest by means of an effective conclusion

What Is Normal, Anyway?

Imagine, for a moment, that everything we take for granted today is gone. Imagine if, instead of hovercars and monobikes, people were forced to travel slow, loud, polluting land-based vehicles capable of little more than one hundred miles an hour. Imagine a life dominated by work—manual labor in positions easily filled by machines. This was the life of 2005. Put yourself in the mindset of someone living two hundred years ago as you read about how those people worked, played, and went between the two. The world of the past is waiting!

If a person went back in time to 2005, the first thing that person would have to do is get somewhere. But how? He or she can't catch the high speed monorail or call a hover-taxi. The most common method of transportation was slow, land-based vehicles called an automobile, or car. These four-wheeled clunkers were driven by gasoline, a highly explosive fuel. If someone wanted to fly to their destination, a non-mach atmosphere-bound "airplane" was the only option. Across the sea, large ships were the only choice, and they took days to cross. Compared to mach-speed, space-capable aerojets and amphibious divers, transportation was, by today's standards, very slow. But for the citizens of 2005, it was as fast as it got.

After someone used one of these methods of transportation, where did he or she go? Most of the time, it was some sort of work. The manual labor which today could easily be completed by an android was done inefficiently by a person. Back then, there were actually people in stores selling their goods! While this seems a waste of a person to us today, there was no A.I. in 2005. People's lives and lifestyles were completely dominated by work. They made their own food—that was work; cleaned the house—also work; and drove themselves from place to place. Now, all these things are done by machines, something the workers of 2005 could only have dreamed about.

Whether working or not, most (but not all) of the people lived in cities. However, they were not like the geometric, plastic metropolis we have now. Most buildings were, at most, about fifty stories high and did not extend underground for more than a few stories. The entire city was usually covered in land-based roads. They were built, quite simply, for cars. In these cities, there were many places for one to buy and eat food. This food, though, was not the time-released mix of vitamins and nutrients we're used to. Much of the food had little nutritional value, and barely anyone had the correct amount of nutrients each day. There were even some people who were too poor to buy food (yes, they had to buy it). Clothing was widely varied, without any resemblance to modern fashion. No one wore a second skin in the cold, and metal on clothing was totally unheard of. While some of it looked okay, none was very successful in protecting the wearer.

Now that you've discovered what the past was like, pause to think about the present. It is different from 2005, yes, but maybe not as much as we think. After all, we were human then, too. Maybe someday, someone will look at us and say that we were underdeveloped and primitive. Maybe someday, 200 years will seem but a miniscule moment in the great history of human civilization.

The "Useful References" section at the back of this book will help you learn more about these other critical features of expository writing:

- Word Choice
- Conventions
- Transitions
- Organizational Patterns
- Titles: Straightforward to Snappy

Specific Revision Criteria for Exposition (Paragraphs and Essays)

Use color-coded highlighters or sticky notes to identify where your expository writing illustrates selected items from the following list of critical features:

Expository Paragraphs

- My explanation includes a clear and specific topic sentence.
- All details in my paragraph relate to the topic I am explaining.
- I include adequate information in my explanation.
- My conclusion emphasizes the importance of the topic or suggests action.
- I use transitions effectively.*

Expository Essays

- My introduction captures the reader's attention by asking a question, presenting an anecdote, explaining an effective quotation, or presenting a foolish or incorrect view.
- My paragraphs develop specific subtopics related to my thesis statement.
- I employ effective transitions among the parts of my essay.*
- I include adequate and interesting information for each subtopic in my explanation.
- The conclusion of my essay is effective in answering questions posed in the introduction, emphasizing a final point, warning the reader, offering a prediction, or suggesting specific action.
- My title informs the reader about the subject of the essay in an interesting way.*

Starred items are features that apply to other writing forms besides expository paragraphs and essays. In the "Useful References" section at the back of this book, check the subsections titled "Transitions" and "Titles: Straightforward to Snappy."

Assessment of Expository Paragraphs and Essays

Use the following rubrics to set personal goals to improve your expository writing. Remember that you can also apply the criteria listed in the generic rubric in Chapter 1.

Expository Paragraph Rubric

	I'm not there yet	I'm getting there	I'm there now
Content	• I need to include additional information in my explanation. • Details in my paragraph are sometimes off-topic.	• I include adequate information in my explanation. • Most details in my paragraph clearly relate to my topic.	• I include detailed information in my explanation. • All details in my paragraph clearly relate to my topic.
Organization	• My paragraph needs a clear topic sentence. • My paragraph needs a strong concluding sentence. • I do not use any transition expressions or techniques in my paragraph.	• I have a topic sentence but it could be stronger. • I include a concluding sentence but it is predictable. • I use transition expressions and techniques but require additional transitions in my paragraph.	• My paragraph includes a clear topic sentence. • My concluding sentence commands attention. • I effectively and adequately use transition expressions and techniques in my paragraph.

Expository Essay Rubric

	I'm not there yet	I'm getting there	I'm there now
Content	• I need to include additional information in my explanation. • Details in my essay are sometimes off-topic.	• I include adequate information in my explanation. • Most details in my essay clearly relate to my topic.	• I include detailed information in my explanation. • All details in my essay clearly relate to my topic.
Organization	• I do not create much interest in my introduction. • My introduction lacks a thesis statement. • My essay lacks transitions. • I abruptly end my essay with no definite conclusion.	• I use rather predictable ways to add interest to my introduction. • My introduction contains a thesis statement. • I have included some transitions but my writing needs more of them. • My conclusion is definite but could be clearer.	• My introduction commands attention. • My introduction contains a clear and effective thesis statement. • I effectively employ transitions among the parts of my essay. • I present a strong and definite conclusion.
Title	• My title provides no guidance about the focus of my explanation.	• While my title informs the reader about the focus of my explanation, it could be more interesting.	• My title informs the reader about the focus of my explanation in an interesting way.

6 Persuasive Writing and Deliberative Inquiry Research

Key Features of Effective Persuasive Writing and Deliberative Inquiry Research

Persuasive writing and deliberative inquiry research deal with issues about which people have different viewpoints. Questions such as "Should students be allowed to use cell phones in school?," "Should the voting age be lowered to 16?," or "How should citizens react to global warming?" will certainly yield many different responses.

While writers will disagree in their responses to such issues, they should be reasonable in expressing their disagreement. The key is to employ facts and reasons to support one's point of view and to be respectful of those who reasonably hold a different point of view.

Persuasive writing seeks to convince the reader of something. This familiar writing form has recently evolved into a related writing form called *deliberative inquiry research*. Over the past few years, deliberative inquiry research has been popular in social studies programs. Deliberative inquiry highlights:

- the exploration of multiple points of view.
- sensitivity to perspectives shared by identifiable groups of people, and demonstrating.
- respect for those who respond in different ways when they make personal decisions about an issue.

Both persuasive writing and deliberative inquiry research emphasize facts and reasons to support personal decisions about issues. However, deliberative inquiry research places greater emphasis on sensitivity and respect. This chapter will focus on deliberative inquiry research.

Planning Strategies for Deliberative Inquiry Research (Paragraphs and Essays)

In this section, you will read about some useful strategies to help you plan a paragraph or essay based on deliberative inquiry research. Begin by making decisions about RAFTS variables.

RAFTS Variables

R	Role	When writing a paragraph or essay involving deliberative inquiry research, you are in the role of a responsible citizen.
A	Audience	You may be writing to a targeted audience, for example, students in your school, your city council, or a government agency responsible for policy decisions. You might also be writing to a general audience consisting of other responsible citizens.
F	Format	Deliberative Inquiry Research. As with other forms of writing, it will be helpful to read examples of effective persuasive writing or deliberative inquiry research before you write in this form.
T	Topic	What is the question or issue that you are examining? The question should lend itself to different viewpoints. For example, "What are voting participation rates in Canada?" is not a deliberative inquiry question since your answer will be factual. On the other hand, "How can we encourage increased voter participation in Canada?" is a deliberative inquiry question.
S	Strong Purpose	Your purpose is to explain your personal decision about a question. You must also support your decision with facts and reasons. In many cases, your purpose will be to invite participation or to recommend a specific course of action.

Using a Modified T-Chart and a Planning Form

When you engage in deliberative inquiry research, you will follow a two-step planning process. Your first step will involve use of a modified T-chart. You will then move on to a planning form for a deliberative inquiry research paragraph or essay.

A T-chart lists pros and cons related to a research question or issue. A modified T-chart includes a column in which to list different sources of opinions or information, along with different viewpoints. This is consistent with the emphasis on multiple perspectives in deliberative inquiry research.

In the example on page 42, a student used a modified T-chart in preparing to respond to the deliberative inquiry research question, "Should the voting age be lowered to 16?" (Note that a blank version of this T-chart appears in the "Reproducible Pages" section at the back of this book.)

Your second step is to employ a planning form for a paragraph or an essay depending on how lengthy your response will be. A student used the Deliberative Inquiry Research Paragraph Planning Form on page 43 to develop a carefully considered personal decision about whether the voting age should be lowered to 16, as well as to organize facts and reasons in response to the research question. (Note that a blank version of this form appears in the "Reproducible Pages" section at the back of this book.)

Modified T-Chart for Deliberative Inquiry Research

Research question: _____

_____

	Pros	Cons
Source 1 Federal politician	Voting rates are down. We need to get young people started on the voting habit. School age children will vote with the benefit of studying political issues in school.	
Source 2 Blogger		16-year-olds are too young to vote. Responsibility comes with age. A study in Germany indicated that voting rates for people aged 16 to 21 fell below the national average.
Source 3 Class survey of 26 students aged 12 to 13	Seventy percent agreed and stated that if 16-year-olds are old enough to drive and work, they should be old enough to vote.	
Source 4 Survey completed by parents/guardians of a class that completed the survey mentioned as Source 3		Sixty-two percent felt that 16-year-olds do not understand issues as well as adults. They need more experience to vote wisely.

Activity

As you read the student's deliberative inquiry research paragraph below, evaluate the following features:

1. How effective is the topic sentence?
2. How effective is the concluding sentence?
3. Does every detail in the body of the paragraph relate to the topic sentence?
4. What might the student have added to the body of the paragraph?
5. What personal decision would you have made about the research question? Explain your answer.

Should the Voting Age Be Lowered to 16?

Sixteen-year-olds should not be allowed to vote. Younger people don't know enough about politics and voting and might make a foolish choice. Many younger people don't care about politics yet or they don't quite understand. Sixteen-year-olds might not look for the most important matters when they vote and vote for someone who wasn't as good as someone else. Eighteen is the prefect voting age because that's when people become an official adult and adults tend to be more responsible. If sixteen-year-olds were allowed to vote, politics would be changed forever.

```
┌─────────────────────────────────────────────────────┐
│         Deliberative Inquiry Research Paragraph       │
│                    Planning Form                      │
│                                                       │
│  Research question:   Should the voting age be lowered to 16?  │
│                                                       │
│                                                       │
│  Topic sentence (directly state your personal decision about the research question):  │
│     Sixteen-year-olds should not be allowed to vote.  │
│                                                       │
│                                                       │
│                                                       │
│                                                       │
│  Facts and reasons that support my personal decision: │
│  · Eighteen is the age when people become official adults. Adults are  │
│    usually more responsible than children.            │
│  · Young people do not have the experience to understand politics as  │
│    well as older people do.                           │
│  · Many young people don't know much about politics and might make a  │
│    foolish choice.                                    │
│  · Sixteen-year-olds might not look for the important matters when they  │
│    vote and end up making a foolish choice.           │
│  · Many young people don't care about politics. Other things are more  │
│    important to them.                                 │
└∿∿∿∿∿∿∿∿∿∿∿∿∿∿∿∿∿∿∿∿∿∿∿∿∿∿∿∿∿∿∿∿∿∿∿∿∿∿∿∿∿∿∿∿∿∿∿∿∿∿∿∿∿∿┘
```

If your deliberative inquiry research requires a more extensive response, use a planning form like the one you would use for expository paragraph writing. The form on page 44 suggests the presentation of different perspectives in the introductory paragraph before a clear statement of your personal decision. Also, the form suggests the use of questions related to the research question as a way to organize your writing. (Note that a blank version of this form appears in the "Reproducible Pages" section at the back of this book.)

Activity

As you read the student's essay on pages 44–45, reflect on these questions:

1. How effectively does the introduction
    a) create interest?
    b) clearly present the inquiry question?
    c) briefly indicate why the question is important?
    d) briefly review different perspectives?

2. How effectively do the supporting paragraphs
    a) present clear topic sentences?
    b) present facts and reasons related to topic sentences?
    c) employ effective transitions?

3. How effective is the final paragraph in emphasizing the strengths and benefits of the writer's personal decision about the question?

4. Do you agree with the writer's personal decision about the deliberative inquiry research question? Explain your answer?

Deliberative Inquiry Research Essay Planning Form

Research question: __To what extent is the Youth Criminal Justice Act__
__fair and equitable?__

Capture attention Explain different perspectives Explain why the issue is important State a personal decision	– The YCJA is very effective in teaching youth a lesson and making sure there are fewer re-offenders. – Dropping crime rates; fewer repeat offenders; consequences for offenders
Topic Sentence (Related question 1) Evidence/Reasons	Youth are at an age where rehabilitation and reintegration are more successful. Separate youth from hardened criminals. Protect privacy for a second chance. Avoid criminal record for young offenders
Topic sentence (Related question 2) Evidence/Reasons	Instead of having a standard punishment for all crimes, the YCJA looks at each case individually.
Topic sentence (Related question 3) Evidence/Reasons	Fair punishments- Consideration of personal history- Consideration of motives
Conclusion (Emphasize a benefit of your personal decision; offer a prediction, a warning, or a suggested action.)	The YCJA is a good law. Stress importance of a compassionate society.

To What Extent Is the Youth Criminal Justice Act Fair and Equitable?

"Nothing is more important than justice and a just society. In this country, we realize that without justice, we have no rights, no peace and no prosperity," says Justice Beverley McLachlin. The YCJA (Youth Criminal Justice Act) was introduced to Canada in 2003. An effective youth criminal justice bill should reduce the rate of crime. The YCJA focuses on providing young offenders with fair punishments that suit the crime while helping them to change their behavior. Some argue that the bill helps young offenders become better, law-abiding citizens; others feel that the justice system should focus more on victims and that punishments should be stricter. Is the Youth Criminal Justice Act fair and equitable? Yes. The YCJA teaches youth a lesson and deters them from re-offending. It makes rehabilitation and reintegration more effective and it looks at each case individually to ensure that fair punishments are given.

First, YCJA is very effective in teaching youth a lesson and making sure there are fewer re-offenders. Statistics prove that since the introduction of YCJA in 2003, the incidence of youth crime has dropped. This proved that YCJA is helping. There are also fewer repeat offenders. Most of the young people who are charged show remorse and are willing to accept the consequences of their crime. They are most often prepared to correct their behavior. In addition, the consequences of crime deter youth from re-offending. These consequences include community service, counseling, and repairing the damage. Offenders realize that their actions were wrong and they learn their lesson. Once they realize that they won't get away with committing a crime without punishment, in most cases, young people do not offend again.

In addition, youth are at an age where rehabilitation and reintegration are more successful. Because adult criminals might potentially have a negative influence on young people, they are kept separate from them. Furthermore, the privacy of young offenders is protected to ensure that they get a second chance. If no one knows who they are, it will be easier for them to reintegrate into society as they more easily continue with their lives. The YCJA also gives youths a second chance to avoid a criminal record, realizing that everyone makes mistakes in growing up. For example, first-time offenders who have committed minor crimes are often able to avoid a criminal record. This gives them a chance to improve their behavior. They are less affected in the future by their crimes.

Instead of having a standard punishment for all crimes, the YCJA looks at each case individually. This ensures that young offenders get fair punishments that fit the crime, punishments such as community service. Any previous records or offences, the age of the accused, the seriousness of the crime, and other factors such as alcohol and substance abuse are taken into consideration. In addition, the court looks at the possible motives for the crime. For some families, essential items are not very easily obtained and this may cause some youths to steal. The court looks at the parents, their jobs, and how often they are at home. For some youths, their parents are seldom at home and so they have no one to teach them proper behavior. When the cases are looked at individually, it creates a sense of equity for individuals.

In conclusion, the YCJA is a good law. It teaches youth a lesson; it makes rehabilitation and reintegration more effective; and it looks at each case individually so that there are fair consequences. It is a vital part of our justice system and helps keep youth in line. The YCJA helps to create a compassionate society.

If you need to learn more about the following features of persuasive writing and deliberative inquiry research, refer to the "Useful Resources" section at the back of this book:

- Word Choice
- Sentence Variety
- Transitions
- Titles: Straightforward to Snappy

Specific Revision Criteria for Deliberative Inquiry Research (Paragraphs and Essays)

Use color-coded highlighters or sticky notes to identify where your deliberative inquiry research (paragraph or essay) illustrates selected items from the following list of critical features:

Deliberative Inquiry Research (Paragraphs)

- I clearly state my personal decision in response to the question.
- I present reasons and facts to support my personal decision.
- My paragraph includes a clear topic sentence.
- My concluding sentence emphasizes the strengths and benefits of my personal decision or ends with a warning, a prediction, or a suggested action.

Deliberative Inquiry Research (Essays)

- I clearly state why the question is important.
- I explain different perspectives about the question.
- I clearly state a logical personal decision about the question.
- I present valid and adequate information and reasoning to support my personal decision.
- I create interest in my opening by asking a question, presenting a startling detail or observation, employing an effective question, or presenting what I regard as a foolish or incorrect view.
- In each paragraph, I use facts, reasons, and proposed actions to clearly develop the topic sentence.
- I include transitions among the parts of the essay.*
- My concluding paragraph emphasizes the benefits of my personal decision, offers a warning, makes a prediction, or suggests a specific action.
- My title informs the reader about the subject of my deliberative inquiry research in an interesting way.*

Starred items are features that apply to other writing forms besides persuasive writing. In the "Useful References" section at the back of this book, check the subsections titled "Transitions" and "Titles: Straightforward to Snappy."

Assessment of Deliberative Inquiry Research (Paragraphs and Essays)

Use the following rubrics to set personal goals to improve your deliberative inquiry research (paragraphs and essays). Remember that you may also apply the criteria listed in the generic rubric in Chapter 1.

Deliberative Inquiry Research Rubric (Paragraph)

	I'm not there yet	I'm getting there	I'm there now
Content	• Readers are not sure about my personal decision. • I give very few facts and reasons or I give some facts and reasons that do not fit my personal decision.	• I express my personal decision but could do so more clearly. • I include just enough facts and reasons to support my personal decision.	• I present a clear and direct statement of my personal decision. • I thoroughly present facts and reasons to support my personal decision.
Organization	• My paragraph needs a clear topic sentence. • My paragraph needs a strong concluding sentence.	• I include a topic sentence but it could be stronger. • I include a concluding sentence but it is predictable.	• My paragraph includes a clear topic sentence. • My concluding sentence commands attention.

Deliberative Inquiry Research Rubric (Essay)

	I'm not there yet	I'm getting there	I'm there now
Content	• I offer little background about the question and perspective. • I am vague in stating my personal decision. • I present little information and evidence related to content. Some information is off-topic.	• I present limited background about the question and only a few perspectives. • I clearly state my personal decision. • I present relevant information and reasoning.	• I clearly establish the importance of the question and present different perspectives. • I emphatically and clearly state my personal decision. • I thoroughly present relevant information and reasoning.
Organization	• I do not create interest in my introduction. • My paragraphs lack definite topics. • I use few transitions among the parts of my essay. • I abruptly end my essay with no definite conclusion.	• I use a predictable way to create interest in my introduction. • Most of my paragraphs focus on a single topic. • I use transitions but could use more of them. • My conclusion is definite but could be stronger.	• My introduction commands attention. • Each of my paragraphs focuses on a single topic. • I effectively employ transitions among the parts of my essay. • I present a strong and effective conclusion.
Title	• My title provides no guidance about the focus of my essay.	• My title informs the reader about the focus of my essay, but it could be more interesting.	• My tile informs the reader about the focus of my essay in an interesting way.

7 Business Letters

Key Features of Effective Business Letters

You can write many types of business letters, including letters of request, invitations, letters to the editor, cover letters for resumés, and claim and adjustment letters. Each type of business letter has a specific purpose:

- A letter of request asks for a favor, a service, an appointment, or an item.
- An invitation requests someone's attendance at an event.
- A letter to the editor expresses the writer's viewpoint about a current item in the news.
- A cover letter for a resumé seeks to motivate an employer to read a resumé by highlighting key points related to a job applicant's qualifications, work experience, and interests.
- A claim and adjustment letter deals with mistakes or perceived mistakes made in business transactions. Customers state claims while businesses write responses called adjustment letters.

All of these types of business letters share several characteristics:

- They should make their purpose clear to the reader.
- They should be concise.
- They should follow a standard business letter format.
- They should be complete and accurate in every detail.
- They should promote goodwill even when the contents of the letter are unpleasant, such as a demand for payment or a complaint about inadequate service.

Planning Strategies for Business Letters

In this section, you will read about some useful strategies to help you plan the writing of a business letter. Begin by making decisions about RAFTS variables.

The first part of an effective business letter focuses on purpose: what you want your reader to understand or to do. Ineffective business letters leave the reader guessing about purpose. An ineffective business letter buries its purpose in the body of the letter. Remember that busy readers are more likely to respond appropriately when you make your purpose clear at the beginning of your business letter.

RAFTS Variables

R	Role	Your role as a business letter writer may vary. Do you represent a group or an organization? Are you in the role of a concerned citizen, a customer with a complaint, or another defined role?
A	Audience	You always have a clearly defined audience in a business letter. Sometimes you need to learn some background information about your audience, for example, when you are applying for a job.
F	Format	What type of business letter are you writing: a letter of request, an invitation, a letter to the editor, a cover letter for a resumé, or a claim and adjustment letter?
T	Topic	What is the subject of your business letter? You need to be very clear about your focus.
S	Strong Purpose	What action are you requesting from your addressee?

Other Planning Strategies for Business Letters

Effective business letters present relevant background information and specify a purpose in the opening paragraph. The middle paragraph or paragraphs present relevant details. The concluding paragraph ends with a goodwill closing.

The B.P.D.O.G. business letter planning form follows this format:

Paragraph one: B (Background) and P (Purpose)

Paragraph two: D (Details) and O (Operations) A detail is a point related to your business letter's purpose. An operation is an action related to the purpose. For instance, if your business letter's purpose is to invite the chairperson of the school council to speak at the graduation ceremony, your second paragraph would include details about the event: time, place, and suggested length of the graduation address. Operations would include information about when the chairperson should arrive and who will meet her. In addition, you would need to specify the requested date of a reply to your invitation.

Paragraph three: G (Goodwill closing)

A student used the form to plan a business letter to nominate a classmate for a citizenship award. (Note that a blank version of this form appears in the "Reproducible Pages" section at the back of this book.)

Activity

As you read the student's business letter, evaluate the following features:

1. How effectively does the opening paragraph present background information and state the purpose of the letter?
2. Would you add or delete anything from the second paragraph? If so, what? Justify your answer.
3. What other possibility might have worked as a goodwill closing to the letter? Explain your answer.

480 River Road
Halifax, Nova Scotia
B7X 2X3

May 15, 2010

Ms. Monica Cardinal
Chairperson
Student Citizen of the Year Committee
Halifax Booster Club
7903 Springfield Avenue
Halifax, Nova Scotia
B2B 1Y9

Dear Ms. Cardinal:

In response to the Booster Club's poster in our school, I am pleased to recommend Marian Tsing for recognition as a student citizen of the year. Marian possesses the qualities of a responsible citizen and leader.

Marian's contributions to her school and community qualify her for the award. She serves as vice president of the Student Council at Clearwater School. In addition, she plays on three school teams—volleyball, basketball, and field hockey. She is captain of the field hockey team. Marian's voluntary community service with the Tiny Tots Swimming Program received recognition in a recent article in *River Heights Community News*. In all of her activities, Marian has demonstrated leadership, cheerfulness, and kindness. I would be pleased to elaborate on my nomination of Marian if you care to contact me at Clearwater School. The telephone number is 555-2300.

Thank you for your consideration of my recommendation.

Sincerely,

Zori Sadeghi

Specific Revision Criteria for Business Letters

After you have checked that you have followed the standard business letter format, use color-coded highlighters or sticky notes to identify where your business letter illustrates selected items from the following list of critical features:

- My first paragraph clearly expresses my purpose.
- My first paragraph presents necessary background information.
- The middle paragraph (or paragraphs) present(s) complete and accurate information.
- The letter concludes with a goodwill closing.
- My word choices are precise and appropriate for my audience.*
- I effectively employ transitions in my business letter.*

Starred items are features that apply to other writing forms besides business letters. In the "Useful References" section at the back of this book, check the subsections titled "Word Choice" and "Transitions."

Assessment of Business Letters

Use the following rubric to set personal goals to improve your business letter writing. Remember that you may also apply the criteria listed in the generic rubric in Chapter 1.

Business Letter Rubric

	I'm not there yet	I'm getting there	I'm there now
Content	• The reader is not sure about my purpose. • My letter lacks details or includes irrelevant details.	• I express my purpose but could be clearer. • I present accurate details but could add at least one critical detail.	• I clearly express my purpose. • I present adequate and accurate details related to my purpose.
Organization	• My business letter does not follow standard business letter format. • My letter lacks clearly organized paragraphs and transitions. • My letter lacks a goodwill closing.	• My business letter mostly follows standard business letter format. • My letter is organized but I could improve use of transitions. • My goodwill closing could be more clearly related to my purpose.	• My business letter is correct in all matters of standard format. • My letter is clearly organized in paragraphs with clear transitions. • My letter concludes with an effective goodwill closing.
Vocabulary	• I am imprecise in some of my word choices. My word choice is sometimes too informal for my audience.	• Most of my word choices are precise and clear. Most of my word choices are appropriate for my audience.	• All of my word choices are precise and clear. All of my word choices are appropriate for my audience.

8 Formal E-mail Messages

Key Features of Effective Formal E-mail Messages

This chapter offers strategies and examples showing how writers compose formal e-mail messages for a range of purposes. It offers specific planning, revision, and assessment strategies related to formal e-mail communication as opposed to informal communication between friends, family members, or participants in a social networking group.

E-mail offers the opportunity for frequent exchanges with family and friends. It is also an important communication tool for conducting business. A formal e-mail message is usually more concise and a bit more conversational than a business letter. However, formal e-mails will be ineffective unless they are carefully written. Unless the e-mail message is well-organized, contains conventional spelling and usage, and features language appropriate to the recipient, it is less likely to get results. Remember that many working people receive mailboxes full of e-mails each day.

An effective formal e-mail message demonstrates the following features:

- The message deals with a single topic.
- The message concisely but completely presents information about the topic.
- The message clearly conveys your purpose for corresponding with the recipient.
- The message clearly indicates action requested on the part of the recipient.
- A formal e-mail message (like all e-mail messages) should be worded respectfully because e-mails can be instantly and widely shared.

Activity

Read the following formal e-mail message sent by a Student Council president to other executive members of the Student Council, with a courtesy copy (Cc) to the council's teacher advisor. Identify the purpose of the e-mail message and the action requested in the message. Note that many computer programs automatically enter the date of an e-mail and identify the sender and the recipient. Identify the advantages and disadvantages that an e-mail message offers the president compared to other forms of communication such as a business letter, an intercom message, a telephone call, or a personal conversation.

To: Lakeview School Student Council Executive
Cc: Ms. Chan, Teacher Advisor
Subject: Emergency Meeting about Welcome Winter Carnival

Dear Student Council Members,

I've just learned that the gymnasium is unavailable for the Welcome Winter Carnival planned for November 27. I've scheduled an emergency Student Council Executive meeting for Tuesday, October 14 in Room A10 at 12:15 p.m. Let's discuss these items at the meeting:

1. rescheduling the carnival

2. advertising and promotion plans

3. contacting volunteers who are organizing activities for the carnival

Let me know whether you can attend.

Thanks.

Pat

Activity

Following the emergency meeting, the president of the Student Council sent an e-mail message to the president of the school's Parents' Council— a person whom the Student Council president had never met. Read the following formal e-mail message. Note any differences in format and content compared to the e-mail message sent to the Student Council Executive members. Make a T-chart in which to record any differences and the reasons for these differences.

To: Mr. John Kozelko, Lakeview School Parents' Council President
Cc: Ms. Chan, Teacher Advisor
Subject: Invitation to the Rescheduled Welcome Winter Carnival

Mr. Kozelko:
Due to a priority booking for our school's gymnasium on November 27, the Welcome Winter Carnival has been rescheduled to December 4, 2009 from 11:30 a.m. to 1:00 p.m. in the gymnasium at Lakeview School.

The Welcome Winter Carnival will feature enjoyable activity centers for students and will raise money for our local children's hospital. Please forward an invitation to all members of the Parents' Council Executive to attend this wonderful traditional event at our school.

Thank you for supporting our Welcome Winter Carnival. Should you have any questions or concerns, contact Ms. Chan at 555-1398.

Please confirm receipt of this message.

Kind regards,
Pat Bennett
President
Lakeview School Student Council
patbennett@realworld.com

Planning Strategies for Formal E-mail Messages

In this section, you will read about some useful strategies to help you plan a formal e-mail message. Begin by making decisions about RAFTS variables.

RAFTS Variables

R	**R**ole	Your role in writing formal e-mail messages will vary. Perhaps you are writing as an employee; a member of a club, organization, or discussion group; a concerned citizen; or a salesperson.
A	**A**udience	Formal e-mail messages should only be sent to those affected by the content of the e-mail message, with a courtesy copy (Cc) to those who need to be aware of the content.
F	**F**ormat	Formal e-mail message. Reread the examples to review how a formal e-mail message is organized. Note how the message is concisely worded and to the point. Note inclusion of specific details related to event, time, place, and the identity and role of the person sending the e-mail message.
T	**T**opic	You should be clear about the topic of a formal e-mail message. State it clearly and briefly in the subject line of the e-mail message. Effective e-mails deal with a single topic that is precisely identified in the subject line.
S	**S**trong Purpose	Formal e-mail messages should clearly inform the recipient of the purpose of the e-mail and indicate any action that you expect the recipient to take.

Other Planning Strategies for Formal E-mail Messages

Remember that formal e-mail messages should deal with a single topic or subject. The formal e-mail should begin with some brief background information and a clear statement of your purpose. The next section should concisely include any relevant information. The message should end with a request for action you wish your recipient or recipients to take.

Remember to avoid using capitalized words in e-mail messages. Doing so is considered shouting in e-mail communication. If you need to emphasize something, use italics or bold text.

A P.I.A. planning form can help you write effective formal e-mail messages. This form consists of the following elements:

P	Purpose	Let your reader know why you are writing the formal e-mail message.
I	Information	Present key details related to your topic and purpose.
A	Action	Indicate the action you are requesting on the part of the recipient.

(Note that a blank version of a P.I.A. planning form appears in the "Reproducible Pages" section at the back of this book.)

Remember to avoid using capitalized words in e-mail messages.
Doing so is considered shouting in
e-mail communication. If you need
to emphasize something, use italics
or bold text.

Specific Revision Criteria for Formal E-mail Messages

On either an online copy or a hard copy of your formal e-mail message, use color-coded highlighting or sticky notes to identify where your formal e-mail succeeds in meeting specific criteria selected from the following list:

- I focus on a single topic, clearly and completely described in the subject line.
- I am concise but complete in my message.
- I introduce myself to recipients I do not know.
- I clearly indicate my purpose at the beginning of my e-mail.
- I clearly indicate action that I am requesting on the part of the recipients.
- I use a standard format for a formal e-mail message.
- I follow common practices related to e-mail etiquette. For example, I use respectful language and I avoid all-capital letters (also known as "flaming"). I keep privacy and confidentiality in mind.

Note: It is important to stop and think before you hit the SEND button. Who should be Cc'd in an e-mail message? Should anyone be blind-copied on a message? Who might be made uncomfortable by a remark contained in an unintended e-mail trail? You might also be surprised to learn that some companies monitor employees' incoming and outgoing e-mail messages.

Assessment of Formal E-mail Messages

Use the following rubric to set personal goals to improve your writing of formal e-mail messages. Remember that you can also apply criteria listed in the generic rubric in Chapter 1.

Formal E-mail Message Rubric

	I'm not there yet	I'm getting there	I'm there now
Content	• My message lacks a focus on a single topic. • My subject line is incomplete in identifying the topic. • The reader is not sure about my purpose. • I do not mention action on the part of the recipient.	• Most of my message deals with the topic of the e-mail. • Mu subject line identifies the topic but could be more specific. • I express my purpose but could be clearer. • I could more clearly indicate action that I am requesting.	• I clearly focus on a single topic. • My subject line clearly and completely identifies the topic. • I clearly express my purpose. • I clearly indicate action that I am requesting.
Organization	• My message does not follow an accepted formal e-mail format. • My message has no clear flow from purpose to information to action.	• My message follows most features of an accepted formal e-mail format. • My message's organization could more clearly show sections related to purpose, information, and action.	• My message follows an accepted formal e-mail format. • My message begins by making the purpose clear, continues with necessary information, and concludes with requested action.
Vocabulary	• My choice of words is inappropriate for my recipient and for the seriousness of the topic.	• My choice of words is appropriate for my recipient and for the seriousness of the topic but I could be more precise.	• My choice of words is consistently appropriate for my recipient and for the seriousness of the topic.
Conventions	• My errors in spelling, punctuation, and usage distract my reader and interfere with the clear expression of my message.	• My one or two errors in spelling, punctuation, and usage are not serious enough to distract my reader.	• I consistently use standard spelling, punctuation, and usage in my message.

9 Reviews of Television and Movie Dramas

Key Features of Effective Reviews of Television and Movie Dramas

This chapter offers strategies and examples that show how writers create powerful reviews of television and movie dramas. It offers specific planning, revision, and assessment strategies related to writing these reviews.

Identifying Genre and Audience

If you took a survey of any age group, you would find that television and movie dramas are popular entertainment options. In fact, such dramas are many people's favorite form of entertainment. Your survey would also reveal that people prefer different types or genres of television and movie dramas. When you write a review of a television or movie drama, your major task is deciding the extent to which you would recommend the drama to viewers. However, there is a wide range of dramas and a wide range of tastes among viewers. Thus, you also need to identify the specific genre of the drama as well as the audience that would most likely enjoy it.

The following lists show a broad range of genres of television and movie dramas. Think of titles that would fit under each genre category as well as genres that you might add to the lists.

Television Drama Genres	Movie Drama Genres
Situation comedy	Action adventure
Soap opera	Comedy
Teen drama	Romance
Children's drama	War drama
Cartoons	Biographical drama
Police and crime drama	Western
Mystery	Historical drama
Historical drama	Biographical drama
Biographical drama	Police and crime drama
Western	Horror
Science fiction	Science fiction
Fantasy	Fantasy

Besides informing readers about the genre, your review should also inform them about the drama's plot and conflicts. The challenge is to include enough detail—

Be sure to read reviews of movie and television dramas in magazines and newspapers as well as on the Internet. Notice how the titles of the reviews are often snappy and imaginative.

but not too much to spoil someone's viewing experience. When you review an episode of a television drama series, your comments about the episode should help readers decide whether the series would interest them or not.

Be sure to read reviews of movie and television dramas in magazines and newspapers as well as on the Internet. Notice how the titles of the reviews are often snappy and imaginative. Notice as well that reviewers usually write with a breezy, conversational voice. Remember that reviewers are not shy in expressing enthusiasm or lack of enthusiasm about a television or movie drama. When they read reviews, readers expect clear and friendly advice about their choices.

Planning Strategies for Reviews of Television and Movie Dramas

In this section, you will read about some useful strategies to help you plan a review of a television or movie drama. Begin by making decisions about RAFTS variables.

RAFTS Variables

R	**R**ole	When you review a television or movie drama, you are in the role of a critic. A critic is someone who expresses a judgment about whether the drama is worth recommending and a judgment about the audience who would enjoy the drama.
A	**A**udience	Since tastes in television and movie dramas differ, you need to be very clear about the audience for your review. If you are writing for a general audience, remember to tell readers about the wide audience appeal of the drama. If you are writing for a clearly targeted audience such as teenagers, think about preferences and background knowledge shared by large numbers of the targeted group. That will help you write a review that connects to their lives and experiences.
F	**F**ormat	Be sure to specify the type or genre of the television series or movie in your review. As mentioned above, read sample reviews in newspapers and magazines before you write your own review.
T	**T**opic	Identify the title of the drama you are reviewing. Remember to write a snappy title for your review.
S	**S**trong Purpose	Your main purpose is to indicate whether you would recommend the drama as well as the audience to whom you would recommend it. Once again, you should inform your reader about the drama's plot and conflicts without giving too much away.

Strategies for Developing and Organizing Your Review

When you review a television or movie drama, try to view it at least twice. Your second viewing will probably lead to critical details and insights that will enhance your review. During or immediately after your viewing, note your impressions and comments in writing. The overview of topics and strategies on pages 59-60 will help you develop and organize your observations and judgments. Not all of these categories need to appear in your review. However, they will certainly help you in your planning.

Reviewing Television and Movie Dramas

Topic	Strategy	Explanation
Background	• Note interesting and relevant background information about the drama—the director, the actors, the subject of the drama, and its source if it is adapted from a novel or another work. A quick Internet search will usually help you locate background information.	• Your review should help readers to connect your comments to what they already know about directors, actors, subjects, and sources. Your background comments will help readers sort out their preferences.
Genre/Subject	• Identify the genre/subject of the drama (e.g., historical fiction, science fiction, horror, romance, western) and comment on the drama's setting and plot.	• Readers' tastes in genres and subjects vary. Information about the drama's setting and plot helps them make viewing choices based on personal interest.
Actors/Acting/ Characters	• Comment briefly on actors in major roles or famous actors in minor roles (cameo performances). Indicate whether you found the acting to be convincing and effective.	• Readers of reviews tend to know a lot about actors and they have their favorites. Readers are interested in the quality of the acting in a television or movie drama.
Conflicts	• Provide a brief overview of the conflicts in the drama.	• The conflicts are the key to how the drama unfolds.
Audience Appeal	• Identify the target audience for the drama. Explain how the drama tries to entertain that audience.	• Many television and movie dramas appeal to specific audiences, for example, special interest groups, adults, or children.

Topic	Strategy	Explanation
Important Images and Sounds	• List images and sounds that were emphasized in the television or movie drama. What emotions did these dominant images and sounds suggest to you?	• As visual and auditory media, television and movie dramas use images and sounds to appeal to emotions. Focusing on images/sounds and related emotions helps you understand and interpret the drama.
Jolts	• List jolts–moments of excitement presented in the television or movie drama (a surprise, a shock, a loud noise, a sudden shift in setting or action) and how each jolt affects you.	• Jolts are an important attention-grabbing technique used in visual media. Identifying them helps you analyze what the film makers wish to emphasize.
Values/Themes	• Analyze the beliefs or attitudes that the drama suggests are important. Are these values worth considering? Why or why not?	• If you pay attention to the subtle messages about values, such as fame, youth, wealth, or success, you will gain clues to audience appeal. Your analysis of themes helps readers to decide whether the drama is focused more on escape or on understanding.

Using a Chart to Plan a Review of a Television or Movie Drama

A blank version of the chart on page 61 is included in the "Reproducible Pages" section at the back of this book. You can use this chart to plan your own review of a television or movie drama. First, note how a reviewer has used the chart to record and organize observations and judgments related to the 2008 television drama, *Journey to the Center of the Earth*. This TV drama is now available on DVD.

Activity

Read the review of *Journey to the Center of the Earth* on pages 61-62 and then answer these questions:

1. What audience does the reviewer suggest for the television drama?
2. How useful is the background information provided in the review? Justify your answer.
3. Is the title effective? Why or why not?
4. Does the review furnish adequate information but not too much information about the actors, characters, conflicts, and themes in the drama?
5. If you have viewed the 2008 version of *Journey to the Center of the Earth*, what changes would you make in the sample review?

Television or Movie Drama Notes

Title: _____ Journey to the Center of the Earth (2008) _____

BACKGROUND	based on 1864 novel by Jules Verne - Verne wanted to show how the world looked when dinosaurs lived - 9 movie versions of this novel have been produced to date
GENRE/SUBJECT	- fantasy. The novel could be considered an early example of science fiction.
ACTORS/ACTING	- Ricky Schroder plays Jonathan Brock – athletic, combative archeologist -Victoria Pratt plays Martha Dennison – wealthy wife of missing explorer - Peter Fonda plays Edward Dennison – missing explorer discovered in lost world - Acting is strong in the movie. Actors are convincing in their roles but there are no stand-outs.
CONFLICTS	- Challenges in locating noted explorer Edward Dennison – missing in Alaska in late 19th century - Challenges throughout – remote location, attacks from dinosaur-like creatures search party captured by tribe in underground world, problem of how to return from underground world to our world
AUDIENCE APPEAL	- Appeals to viewers who like action adventures - Appeals to young adults
IMPORTANT IMAGES	- Darkness throughout movie creates terror, suspense. - Foggy setting in wilderness creates frightening atmosphere.
JOLTS	Boxing match opens movie – shows Brock as tough and stubborn. - Skeleton discovered in tunnel – shows danger of journey. - Attack by prehistoric creatures – shows world of dinosaurs. - Switch from darkness to light in underworld – shows world within a world
VALUES	- Toughness and determination as well as scientific knowledge are needed to make exciting discoveries. - Respect for different cultural traditions. - Understanding of world during the age of dinosaurs. - Issue about whether scientific discoveries should sometimes be kept secret.

Journey to the Center of the Earth—Retro Indiana Jones

Indiana Jones, the combative archeologist featured in several wildly popular movies, has a mid-nineteenth century double in Jonathan Brock, an athletic and aggressive archeologist in *Journey to the Center of the Earth*. Based on Jules Verne's 1864 novel, the film emphasizes one of Verne's major goals: to portray the Earth as it was during dinosaur times. However, the 2008 movie version, directed by T.S. Scott, moves to other themes that are more familiar to modern movie audiences.

Ricky Schroder stars as Jonathon Brock, the athletic archeologist hired by Martha Dennison (played by Victoria Pratt) to locate her missing husband, the explorer Edward Dennison (played by Peter Fonda). These three characters offer convincing performances in this fantasy adventure. In fact, the acting is one of the television drama's strongest production features.

In search of Edward Dennison, Brock and Martha Dennison assemble a crew and follow clues that lead them to Alaska (changed from Iceland in the Verne novel) and through an amazing passage to the center of the Earth. Life-threatening conflicts including loss of horses in the remote wilderness, dangerous terrain in underground passages, and attacks from dinosaur-like creatures keep viewers in constant suspense.

Furthermore, the movie effectively develops terror in the audience with several scenes in dark and foggy settings and with jolts including discovery of an explorer's skeleton and attacks from inhabitants of the center-Earth world.

Despite the non-stop adventure, *Journey to the Center of the Earth* suggests themes familiar to modern audiences, for example, respect for different cultures and the need for scientists to be strong and determined as well as scholarly. The film raises the question about whether scientific knowledge should sometimes be hidden from a world that isn't ready for it.

Young viewers who love fantasy and adventure will be the most appreciative audience of *Journey to the Center of the Earth*. If you like Indiana Jones, you'll certainly like Jonathan Brock and you'll certainly enjoy his unexpected adventures.

Important Features of Reviews of Television and Movie Dramas

If you need to learn more about the following important features of television and movie drama reviews, check the "Useful References" section at the back of this book. You will probably find it easier to include these features in your review once you have completed a first draft.

- Word Choice
- Transitions
- Titles: Straightforward to Snappy

Specific Revision Criteria for Reviews of Television and Movie Dramas

Use color-coded highlighters or sticky notes to identify where your writing illustrates important characteristics of television or movie drama reviews. If any of these characteristics are missing in your review, revise your writing to include them.

- I have provided interesting and relevant background information about the television or movie drama.
- I have identified the type or genre of the drama and provided brief information about its plot.
- I have included a concise overview of important characters and conflicts. I have indicated the target audience for the drama.
- I have mentioned major actors and commented on the quality of their performances.
- I have commented on values and themes suggested by the drama.
- I have clearly indicated whether or not I would recommend the television or movie drama.
- I provided details from the drama to support my observations and judgments.

Assessment of Reviews of Television and Movie Dramas

Use the following rubric to set personal goals to improve your writing of reviews of television and movie dramas. Remember that you can also apply the criteria listed in the generic rubric in Chapter 1.

Rubric for a Review of a Television or Movie Drama

	I'm not there yet	I'm getting there	I'm there now
Content	• I include inadequate information about the drama's plot, genre, and target audience. • I provide an inadequate overview of important characters and conflicts. • My review provides little or no description of values and themes suggested by the drama. • My review does not include a judgment or recommendation.	• I include some brief and important information about the drama's plot, genre, and target audience. • I provide a sketchy overview of important characters and conflicts. • My review describes values and themes suggested by the drama but could do so more clearly. • My review indicates the extent of my recommendation but could do so more clearly and with more details to support my judgment.	• I include adequate, brief, and important information about the drama's plot, genre, and target audience. • I provide an adequate overview of important characters and conflicts. • My review clearly describes values and themes suggested by the drama. • My review clearly indicates the extent of my recommendation and includes adequate details to support my judgment.
Organization	• My writing is disorganized.	• My writing is arranged logically but I could improve the transitions.	• My writing has a logical structure and effective transitions.
Voice	• My writing is wooden with little indication of my attitude toward the television or movie drama.	• I could be more consistent in conveying my attitude toward the television or movie drama.	• My attitude toward the television or movie drama is clearly evident.
Title	• My title provides no information about the drama I am reviewing.	• My title introduces the television or movie drama but could be more imaginative.	• My title imaginatively introduces the television or movie drama.

10 Exploratory Writing

Key Features of Exploratory Writing

Suppose someone asked you why people write and why it is important to write well. You would probably answer that we write to communicate with others and that we need to write well to communicate effectively. While writing to communicate is critical, we write for other important reasons as well. For example, we write to develop understanding of a subject, to reflect about something, or to make personal connections. Sometimes this exploratory writing leads to formal writing. Sometimes it does not. Learning logs and personal responses to literature are common examples of exploratory writing that are probably familiar to you.

Learning Logs

Learning logs give you an opportunity to improve your learning in any subject. For example, at regular intervals when studying topics such as "photosynthesis" or "tyranny," you can take a few minutes to write about your current understanding. Your writing will help you to recall important points, to recognize what you're not sure about, and to set goals for further learning. Many students use graphic organizers or diagrams as well as words in their learning logs. Using graphics is a valuable strategy because visual representations are often helpful aids to learning.

When using a learning log, you might include some of the following features in your entries:

- Summaries
- Familiar examples
- Questions
- Connections to what you already know
- Comments
- Predictions
- Illustrations
- Observations
- Points of uncertainty
- Comments about how your understanding is changing
- Learning goals

Over time, try to include as many of these features in your entries as you can and try to be as detailed as possible. A student completed the learning log entry on page 65 following a guest speaker's presentation on healthy lifestyle choices.

Students made jot notes during the presentation before completing learning log entries. The student's teacher challenged the class to identify a personal goal related to the presentation.

Activity

Read the following learning log entry. Which learning log features from the list on page 64 are represented in the entry? Discuss answers to this question with a partner.

Learning Log Entry: Healthy Lifestyle Choices

Dr. Perez talked about lots of items related to a healthy lifestyle. She started with the do's and went on to the don'ts. Do eat healthy foods (less trans fats/ less fast foods/more fruits and veggies); exercise at least three times a week. See your doctor at least once a year and check on your vaccinations. Don't smoke or drink alcohol; drugs aren't cool. She talked about attitude: staying positive, laughing, sharing time with friends, etc. I'm sorry she didn't talk more about depressed kids. I wondered what she'd have to say but there wasn't time for questions. Too bad. I liked what she said about benefits like having more energy and avoiding being sick if you make good choices. It made me think about eating better. That's my goal.

Personal Responses to Literature

Personal written responses to literature share some characteristics with learning logs, but these responses place greater emphasis on emotional reactions to what you are reading. In written responses to literature, you might include the following items:

- Questions
- Comments
- Predictions
- Suggested possibilities
- Observations
- Points of uncertainty
- Favorite parts
- Favorite characters
- Similarities to other texts
- Understandings developed by the text
- Familiar places and characters the book reminds you of
- People you know who would like and who would not like this text

Over time, try to include many of these items in your writing and try to be as detailed as possible.

Activity

Read the written response to literature on page 66 and then answer these questions.

1. Identify the kinds of thinking that the student includes in the response.
2. Identify where the student could add details to the response to make it even stronger.

Personal written responses to literature share some characteristics with learning logs, but these responses place greater emphasis on emotional reactions to what you are reading.

January 13

Response to *Cages of Glass, Flowers of Time* by Charlotte Culin

1.   I wondered about what the title is supposed to mean. Perhaps *Cages of Glass* means that the protagonist, Claire, is in her own cage because she is afraid of the outside world as well as afraid of people. After all, Claire is abused and neglected. "Glass" refers to what she can see around her but she is still in a cage because she can't reach out.

2.   I'm not sure about the *Flowers of Time* part of the title. In preview entries, I talked about some stories being long. This one was long. I enjoyed it even though there was too much repetition for me. I reacted differently to different characters because Culin described them so well. For example, Claire was frightened of everything. The description of her running away from people and hiding from them helped me understand. I like the book but I need to talk to someone about the *Flowers of Time* part of the title.

Planning Strategies for Exploratory Writing

In this section, you will read about some useful strategies to help you plan a piece of exploratory writing. Begin by making decisions about RAFTS variables.

RAFTS Variables

R	**R**ole	You complete learning logs and personal written responses to literature for yourself—for your own learning and your own understanding.
A	**A**udience	While you sometimes share entries with others, you are your own primary audience when you engage in exploratory writing. When you share entries with your teacher or someone else, your sharing will focus on helping you learn rather than assessing your work.
F	**F**ormat	A type of exploratory writing such as a learning log entry or a written response to literature.
T	**T**opic	In learning logs, the entry is the topic or concept you are studying. In written responses to literature, your topic is the text that you are reading.
S	**S**trong Purpose	Your purpose is to develop your understanding. Taking risks and varying the type of thinking in your entries will help you develop understanding.

Other Planning Strategies for Exploratory Writing

Here are three other strategies you can apply during the planning stage of your exploratory writing.

Take Jot Notes

Your exploratory writing will certainly be more productive if you employ helpful strategies in the discussion and reading you do before you complete your entries.

If you tend to lose focus during pre-sentations and lessons, learn to take jot notes to help you.

If you tend to lose focus during presentations and lessons, learn to take jot notes to help you. Teachers and guest speakers often begin with an overview of the lesson or presentation. If you write down the key topics in jot-note form, you can use your jot notes to organize information presented later.

Employ Reading Strategies

Your teacher will help you learn about reading strategies. Discover the ones that work best for you. Many students stress the value of visualizing, predicting, questioning, and summarizing as strategies that help them comprehend a text.

Vary Your Responses

From the lists of features and items presented in this chapter, choose the learning log entry and the response to literature suggestions that are most useful in helping you to learn and to think. With classmates, you might examine the lists to suggest additional items.

Vary the items that you choose from the lists from entry to entry. For instance, if you usually write summaries in learning log entries, think about including predictions and questions as tools to help you learn and think about your topic.

Specific Revision Criteria for Exploratory Writing

Since exploratory writing emphasizes learning rather than communicating, revision of exploratory writing has a different purpose. Instead of changing the text to communicate effectively, you are reflecting on how to set goals to improve your exploratory writing. Your focus is on how to learn and think more effectively.

For a collection of entries, use your lists of exploratory writing possibilities and a sticky note to mark the various kinds of entries you have written. Use another sticky note to mark your most detailed entry. Use a third sticky note to set a goal for future exploratory writing.

Assessment of Exploratory Writing

Use this rubric to set goals related to the varied features, the details, and the frequency of your learning log entries and written responses to literature. Since exploratory writing focuses on learning and thinking rather than communicating, you do not need to apply the criteria listed in the generic rubric in Chapter 1. Focus on your learning and thinking instead!

Exploratory Writing Rubric

	I'm not there yet	I'm getting there	I'm there now
Varied features	• I need to include a greater variety of thinking in my entries.	• I show some variety in the kind of thinking I included in my entries.	• I show extensive variety in the kind of thinking I included in my entries.
Details	• I need to add details to my entries.	• I include adequate details in my entries.	• I include plenty of details in my entries.
Frequency	• I have completed few of the required exploratory writing entries.	• I have completed most of the required exploratory writing entries.	• I have completed all of the required exploratory writing entries.

Useful References

The information in this section will help you learn about important features of writing in more than one writing form. Revisit this section as often as you wish for help with useful techniques to apply as you experiment with different forms of writing.

Word Choice

In all the writing that you do, your word choice should be precise and accurate. If you are not sure about the meaning of a word, check a dictionary before you use the word.

In all your writing as well, you should consider your audience in your choice of words. For instance, suppose you are a scientist writing an article for a popular science magazine or website. You would include definitions, examples, and illustrations for readers who are non-scientists that scientists would not need in order to understand the scientific vocabulary you are using.

When you write stories, poems, and descriptions, you select words to convey emotional meanings as well as the literal meanings of the words. For example, you convey a more positive emotional meaning when you write about returning to your "home" rather than returning to your "apartment." Writers need to remember that words should help readers visualize the characters, places, and events in the stories, poems, and descriptions that they read. What do you visualize when you read the following sentences?

- The thief went into the parlor.
- The hooded thief went into the parlor.
- The hooded thief sneaked into the parlor.
- The hooded thief quietly sneaked into the empty parlor.

Note how adjectives such as "hooded," adverbs such as "quietly," and colorful verbs such as "sneaked" aid your visualization of the event. Be careful to avoid adding words that do not aid the reader's visualization. For example, "The hooded thief quietly sneaked into the empty, deserted, vacant parlor" is wordy. Consider the student's choice of the word "parlor." How would you visualize the scene differently if the student had written "living room"?

In the following student writing sample, identify three examples of effective word choice—especially words that help readers to visualize. Then suggest one word change that would help the reader visualize something more clearly.

In the valley, the little town of Binkeyville was calm as Junior sat on top of Nulls Hill. The remarkable tree on top of the enormous hill was swaying in the wind. The hand-sized leaves provided shade for Junior as he thought for hours until his head throbbed.

His gray eyes glistened in the sun as he stared into the light, blue sky. His blond hair was tangled in the misty grass as he lay there under his favorite tree. His plump arms were crossed behind his head. Colorful butterflies rested on the tall dandelions and Junior quietly observed them.

Junior often went to the center of this quaint town to think. He had been given a project by his teacher, Mrs. Gush, to research a topic of his choice. He was to write a five-page report with his findings. Junior thought his project was going to be difficult. After all, he was only in the fourth grade.

Conventions

By respecting a standard system for spelling, punctuation, capitalization, word use, and grammar/usage, we communicate more clearly and efficiently in our writing.

Conventions refer to standard use of language. By respecting a standard system for spelling, punctuation, capitalization, word use, and grammar/usage, we communicate more clearly and efficiently in our writing. For example, if we use the apostrophe correctly in "the students' challenges," we know that more than one student faces the challenges. On the other hand, if we write "the student's challenges," we are referring to just one student. If we misuse this convention, we will confuse our readers.

In a school district's marking session focused on middle school writing samples, teachers identified the following instances of unconventional writing as frequent challenges for students:

- Incorrect capital letters
- Incorrect use of apostrophes
- Sentence fragments
- Run-on sentences
- Incorrect use of quotation marks
- Sudden switch from complete sentences to point form
- Misuse of "who," "which," and "what"
- Confusion of "its" and "it's"
- Confusion of "there," "their," and "they're"
- Switch in role (for example, from "I" to "you")
- Switch from past tense to present tense

Activity

How many of the instances listed above present personal challenges for you as a writer? With a partner or in a small group, discuss the conventions that you find especially challenging and brainstorm strategies for dealing with these challenges.

Tips for Learning Conventions

Since handbooks of grammar and usage present many pages of advice about conventional usage, you may become overwhelmed. For instance, some handbooks present more than 25 rules for conventional use of the comma! Your teacher will probably offer instruction about matters of convention that challenge many students in the class. However, it is important that you take ownership for your own challenges in using conventions. The following advice should help you.

1. Keep a personal writing goals chart as recommended in Chapter 1 of this book. While your list will include many items other than conventions, goals that include conventions, such as "Improve sentence variety," should be part of your ambitions to become a better writer.
2. Set priorities. Focus on avoiding mistakes that occur frequently in your writing.
3. Work efficiently. Your teacher will recommend reference books that promote learning about specific challenges in using conventions. Use these references to learn about conventional language use related to your personal writing goals. Consider completing practice exercises related to your personal goals. Don't forget to rewrite sentences from your own writing in which a particular mistake occurred.
4. Edit your next composition with your personal goals in mind and make checking for conventions a priority.
5. Keep a "Spelling Demons" list for the words you frequently misspell in your compositions. Ask your teacher to help you set priorities. Frequently used words represent an obvious priority for standard spelling. The following three-step strategy has helped many students take ownership for personal spelling challenges:
   a) Copy out the misspelled word with the misspelled part included.
   b) Close your eyes and picture the word spelled correctly. Write out the correctly spelled word five times.
   c) Re-write the sentence in which the misspelled word occurred. This time, spell the word correctly.

Sentence Variety

Sentence variety adds interest to writing. Moreover, it shows how parts of a sentence are connected—how the less important parts relate to the more important parts. You can add interest and clarity to your writing if you vary your sentence patterns and types.

Sentence Patterns

A typical sentence begins with a subject, as in these two sentences: "The batter marched confidently to the plate. He hit a home run." Note four ways to add variety by combining these sentences:

- After the batter marched confidently to the plate, he slammed a home run.
- Marching confidently to the plate, the batter slammed a home run.
- Up to the plate the batter marched before he slammed a home run.
- Confidently marching to the plate, the batter hit a home run.

Examine these patterns more closely:

- The first sentence begins with a subordinate clause. Subordinate clauses begin with words such as "after," "when," "although," "before," "since," "unless," and "while."
- The second sentence begins with a participle—a word ending in "ing"—such as "marching," "running," "creeping," "hoping," and "singing."
- The third sentence begins with a prepositional phrase: "up to the plate." Here are a few other examples of prepositions that are used in prepositional phrases: "on," "in," "under," "below," "across," "over," "from," and "after."
- The fourth sentence begins with an adverb (often a word ending in "ly," such as "confidently"). Here are a few examples of adverbs: "slowly," "clearly," "reluctantly," and "happily."

Sentence Types

You can add variety to your writing by incorporating different sentence types, as shown below:

- Most sentences are declarative. "It's sunny today." is a declarative sentence.
- Sentences that pose a question are interrogative: "Is it sunny today?"
- Sentences that express emotion are exclamatory: "I am thrilled that it's sunny today!"
- Sentences that give an order or a command are imperative: "Wish for a sunny day for our picnic."

Activity

Read the following student writing sample and then answer the questions. Combine two sentences in the sample so that the new sentence does not begin with a subject. Determine where you could effectively add a different sentence type to the paragraph. Rewrite the paragraph and include the additional sentence.

Memories

My favorite memories are definitely my family vacations. My favorite vacation was our trip to Texas. We saw a snake out of the car window. We got to eat rattlesnake at a country restaurant. We drove all the way from Austin to the Barrier Island in the Gulf of Mexico. I swam in the ocean. It was full of jellyfish but I didn't care. I enjoyed the trip because what I saw and what I got to do was so different.

Transitions

The parts of your composition should be clearly connected to each other so that they are reader-friendly.

The parts of your composition should be clearly connected to each other so that they are reader-friendly. To connect parts of your text smoothly, use two techniques:

1. Refer to a previous point. For instance, if you have already written about three sources of pollution, a later mention of "these pollution sources" would strengthen the transition among the parts of your writing.
2. Use familiar transition expressions, including the ones on the following page.

Sequence: first, next, later, furthermore, last
Location: below, above, near, farther on, to the left
Similarity: likewise, similarly, again, moreover
Difference: however, in contrast, nevertheless, regardless, on the other hand
Illustration: for example, for instance, of course, to illustrate
Cause and effect: as a result, therefore, thus, consequently

Vary your transition expressions. For example, if you have four key points, instead of transition expressions such as "first," "second," "third," and "fourth," consider a pattern such as "first," "in addition," "moreover," and "most importantly."

Activity

Read the following sample of student writing and then answer the questions.
1. Find and list as many transition expressions as you can that the writer of the sample uses.
2. Identify a place in the writing sample in which the writer uses a reference to a previous point as a transition.
3. Determine which transition expression you could add to the final paragraph to make it more effective.
4. Share your suggestion with a partner.

My First Walk Home from School

Five years ago when I was in kindergarten, I had to walk home for the first time. My friend Angela and I were best friends who played together at every recess. Angela walked with me.

One day parents from neither family came to pick us up from school. Each family thought that the other had agreed to the pick-up. We waited and waited but no one arrived. Angela suggested that we walk. I wasn't sure but away we went. An hour later we were wandering lost along a railway track. Next I noticed my dad's blue car on a nearby road. I waved and fortunately my dad noticed us and stopped.

Everybody in both families apologized and said how relieved they were. Angela and I kept quiet. We didn't know we were in danger and we enjoyed our adventure.

Organizational Patterns

Choose the most logical pattern of organization for your writing. For example:

- If you present details and reasons in an expository paragraph, build to your strongest point.
- If you are writing a sequence of steps such as a recipe or directions to a mall, be certain that you present all steps in the correct order.
- If you are presenting a sequence of events, you will usually follow a time sequence unless you are consciously using a flashback or flash-forward technique.
- If you are describing a scene, choose a point in the scene as you smoothly "pan" or move to other important details.

If you are explaining a problem, a solution, and the result of the chosen solution, use a planning chart for your writing like the one shown below. (Note that a blank version of this chart appears in the "Reproducible Pages" section at the back of this book.)

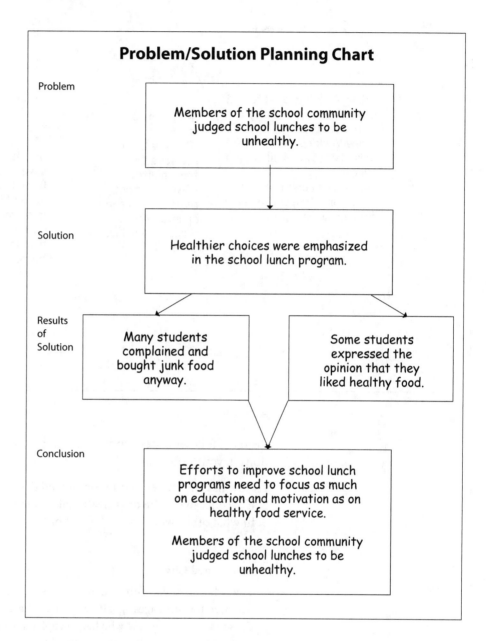

If your expository writing or descriptive writing involves comparison and contrast, use a Venn diagram. For example, the following Venn diagram compares Tokyo and New York City. (Note that a blank version of this Venn diagram appears in the "Reproducible Pages" section at the back of this book.)

Venn Diagram

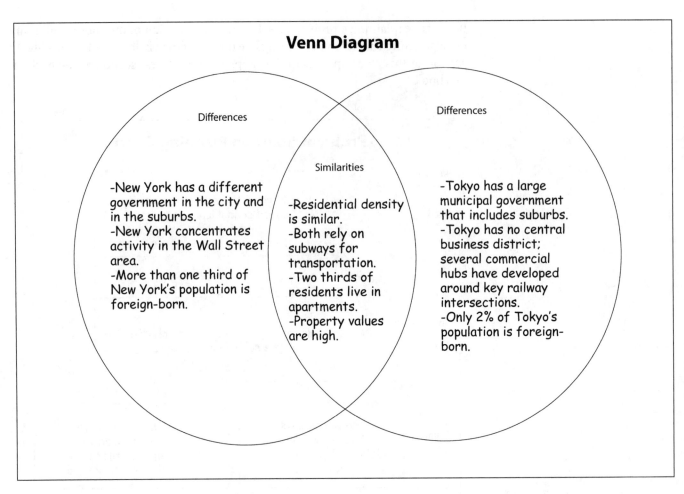

Differences

Similarities

Differences

-New York has a different government in the city and in the suburbs.
-New York concentrates activity in the Wall Street area.
-More than one third of New York's population is foreign-born.

-Residential density is similar.
-Both rely on subways for transportation.
-Two thirds of residents live in apartments.
-Property values are high.

-Tokyo has a large municipal government that includes suburbs.
-Tokyo has no central business district; several commercial hubs have developed around key railway intersections.
-Only 2% of Tokyo's population is foreign-born.

Activity

Read the following description written by a student and then answer these questions in your notebook.

1. How has the student writer organized details in the description?
2. How effective is the organizational pattern? Justify your answer.
3. In what other ways could the author have organized the description? Explain your answer.

Abandoned City

The old stone walls crumbled down the steep mountain. The mysterious city had been forsaken ages ago. If you listened hard enough, you could almost hear the sounds of the people who had occupied the city decades ago. I waited, for it seemed that the people of the city would appear at any moment. Carved into the mountain stood a large structured city. Stairways led here and there and stone buildings were scattered around.

The wind whipped my hair around my face as I climbed the stone staircase to the top of the mountain. The view was magnificent. The wind ceased its insistent gusting for a moment and silence enclosed me. It seemed that all motion ceased and the mountain became empty and desolate.

I examined the city. It had been expertly carved into the mountain and stones had been taken to build walls. Bad weather had eroded smaller forts, which were to the left of the mountain. I smiled and sighed at the peaceful setting.

As suddenly as the wind had stopped, it picked up again, compelling me to walk down the old staircase. I strolled over to my car which seemed obsolete in this ancient city. I left without a backward glance, back to civilization.

Activity

Read the following paragraph. Evaluate whether it is logically organized. Rewrite the paragraph to show improved organization.

Friends and Family

I enjoy my friends and family. My very best friend is Sunita Singh who lives next door. I have four members in my family. My brother, Paul, is 11 going on 12. My mom and dad are both accountants. All members of my family enjoy swimming. All of my friends attend my school. Arash, Danielle, and Kim play video games with me. My grandmother and grandfather are special to me. Life would be dull without these special people.

Besides adding at least one original comparison, revise your writing to ensure that you have not used clichés.

Comparisons: From Clichés to Originality

By including at least one original comparison in your writing, you add a distinct voice to your writing—a personal touch that distinguishes you from other writers. Besides adding at least one original comparison, revise your writing to ensure that you have not used clichés. Clichés are overused and wornout expressions and comparisons such as "upset the apple cart," "all thumbs," "taken to the cleaners," "opening a can of worms," "like two peas in a pod," and "without batting an eye." When you locate a cliché in your writing, rewrite it. Remember that clichés are the greatest enemy of voice in your writing.

To express surprise, a student wrote the following original comparison:

- My eyes opened as wide as avocado pits.

To express happiness, another student wrote the following:

- I smiled a half-moon smile.

You may not feel that you can be as imaginative as these students in their ability to create original comparisons. However, you can learn to avoid clichés and strive to create fresh comparisons. A helpful way to create originality in making comparisons is to employ a comparison frame such as the one on page 76. (Note that a full-sized reproducible version of this chart appears in the "Reproducible Pages" section at the back of this book.)

Using a comparison frame, students added originality to these comparisons:

- John was as frustrated as the hockey forward who has not scored in ten games.
- Larry was as hungry as a bear that had just awakened from hibernation.
- Their conversation boomed like the noise in the school hallway that clearly signals the start of summer break.

Comparison Frame

_____ as/like _____

_____

_____

_____

who/that _____

_____

_____

Notice how the comparison frame helps you add originality by adding detail to what might be an ordinary comparison. "Hungry as a bear" is a cliché, but "hungry as a bear that has just awakened from hibernation" is much more original by comparison.

Activity

In the following description titled "On My Bike" written a by a student, identify two comparisons.
1. Which comparison is the more original of the two? Justify your answer.
2. Which comparison uses the comparison frame? How does the comparison frame succeed in adding originality to the description?

On My Bike

The moisture-deprived fall air evaporated the perspiration on my wind-swept face, as I raced headlong down the dusty gravel path. Despite the dilapidated condition of the bike on which I sat, I still hugged corners, like a hovercraft skimming the breakers, with a rush of adrenaline, a rush that could be provided by few other activities. As the dead leaves became even deader with a crunch, crinkle, snap, and I rocketed further down the twisted abyss of speed and motion, my overworked heart pulsated more laboriously. An unavoidable weariness began to hang over me, like a blackened storm cloud that was heavy with thunder. My aching hamstrings and overheated body were not what they were five minutes ago… had it been five minutes? It seemed like centuries. So I hopped off my bike, and wondered why I had been compelled to get on in the first place.

Titles: Straightforward to Snappy

Titles should give readers a sense of the topic you have chosen for your writing while also creating interest in your text at the same time. Examine the chart on page 77 showing some titles created for pieces of student writing.

Titles should give readers a sense of the topic you have chosen for your writing while also creating interest in your text at the same time.

Title	Subject
Our New-Found-Land	Our family's first trip to Newfoundland
Cancer in the Family	Dealing with a cancer diagnosis
Want to Know a Secret?	Explanation about why we have trouble keeping secrets
The Top Five Tips in Your Part-time Job Search	Job-hunting strategies
Should the voting age be lowered to 16?	Argument stating that the voting age should not be lowered to 16
Frightmare	Poem about bad dreams
Pet Peeves	Humorous writing about what pets might say about their owners
Fool Me Once—Shame on You	Explanation about why people lie
Take Better Pictures	Advice about taking better photographs
Freedom and Peanut Butter	Story about someone who enjoys simple pleasures
Mother Teresa—Saintly Simplicity	Biography of Mother Teresa
Hockey Sticks Are Personal	Poem about favorite objects

Serious subjects usually mean that the title you create for your writing piece will be relatively straightforward. Still, you can add interest to a straightforward title, as shown below.

• Make the reader wonder	• Cancer in the Family
• Ask a question	• Should the Voting Age be Lowered to 16?
• Focus your readers' attention	• The Top Five Tips for Your Part-Time Job Search
• Appeal to your readers' interests	• Take Better Pictures

If your writing is personal and less serious, a snappier title may be appropriate, for example:

• Use a quotation or a popular saying	• Fool Me Once—Shame on You
• Use a pun	• Our New-Found-Land
• Surprise or shock the reader	• Hockey Sticks Are Personal
	• Freedom and Peanut Butter

Sometimes a writer can employ the same technique to create an attention-grabbing title for both serious and less serious subjects. For example, a writer can use alliteration (repetition of the first consonant of two or more words) to generate an interesting title, such as:

Pet Peeves
Mother Teresa—Saintly Simplicity

Reproducible Pages

My Personal Writing Goals

Goals Identified	Goals Achieved

Pre-Writing Form for Planning a Description

Topic (Scene or Event): _____

Emotional Reaction: _____

Sight	Sound	Touch	Smell	Taste

Pembroke Publishers. © 2010 *The Writing Triangle* by Graham Foster. ISBN 978-1-55138-259-3

Planning Frame for Narrative Writing

TITLE: _____

MAIN CHARACTER: _____

SETTING (where/when your story takes place): _____

CONFLICT (the problem your main character must deal with) : _____

_____

_____

CONSEQUENCE OF THE CONFLICT (the effects of the conflict on your main character; show details):

_____

_____

_____

_____

_____

_____

CLIMAX (the resolution of the conflict) : _____

_____

ENDING (an indication of what has changed for the main character or for another character):

_____

_____

_____

Pembroke Publishers. © 2010 *The Writing Triangle* by Graham Foster. ISBN 978-1-55138-259-3

Showing Emotions in a Story

Examples of Emotions:

Excitement
Joy
Fear
Anger
Relief
Hatred
Jealousy
Love
Pity
Sadness

Emotion being portrayed: _____

Show your character's emotion by including details that are related to the following:

Your character's hair, mouth, eyes, and body:

Sounds or movements made by your character:

Something your character says and how it is said:

Your character's breathing and heart rate:

Your character's actions:

Pembroke Publishers. © 2010 *The Writing Triangle* by Graham Foster. ISBN 978-1-55138-259-3

Expository Paragraph Planning Form

Purpose: _____

Topic sentence: _____

_____

_____

Information I could use in my paragraph with the most important point starred:

_____

_____

_____

_____

_____

_____

_____

_____

_____

_____

_____

_____

Concluding sentence: _____

_____

Pembroke Publishers. © 2010 *The Writing Triangle* by Graham Foster. ISBN 978-1-55138-259-3

Expository Essay Planning Form

Purpose: _____

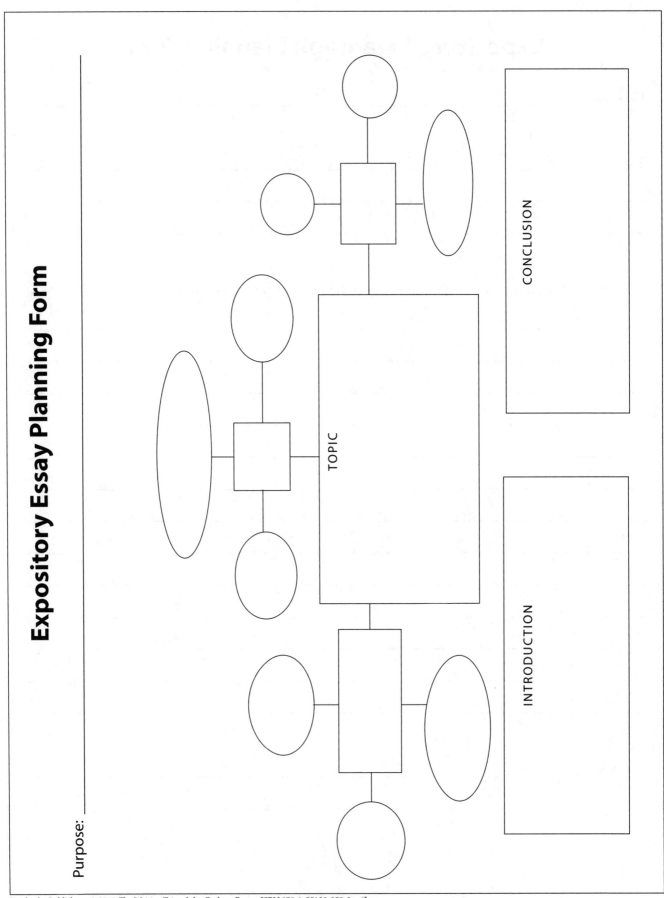

TOPIC

INTRODUCTION

CONCLUSION

Modified T-Chart for Deliberative Inquiry Research

Research question: _____

_____

	Pros	Cons
Source 1		
Source 2		
Source 3		
Source 4		

Deliberative Inquiry Research Paragraph Planning Form

Research question: _____

Topic sentence (directly state your personal decision about the research question):

_____

_____

_____

Facts and reasons that support my personal decision:

_____

_____

_____

_____

_____

_____

_____

_____

_____

_____

Concluding sentence (present a strong final point, a prediction, or a warning, or suggest a specific action):_____

_____

_____

_____

Pembroke Publishers. © 2010 *The Writing Triangle* by Graham Foster. ISBN 978-1-55138-259-3

Deliberative Inquiry Research Essay Planning Form

Research question: _____

_____

Capture attention

Explain different perspectives

Explain why the issue is important

State a personal decision

Topic Sentence (Related question 1)

Evidence/Reasons

Topic sentence (Related question 2)

Evidence/Reasons

Topic sentence (Related question 3)

Evidence/Reasons

Conclusion (Emphasize a benefit of your personal decision; offer a prediction, a warning, or a suggested action.)

Pembroke Publishers. © 2010 *The Writing Triangle* by Graham Foster. ISBN 978-1-55138-259-3

B.P.D.O.G. Planning Form for Business Letters

B	Background:
P	Purpose:
D	Details/Operations:
O	
G	Goodwill closing:

Pembroke Publishers. © 2010 *The Writing Triangle* by Graham Foster. ISBN 978-1-55138-259-3

P.I.A. Planning Form for Formal E-Mail Messages

P	Purpose:
I	Information:
A	Action:

Pembroke Publishers. © 2010 *The Writing Triangle* by Graham Foster. ISBN 978-1-55138-259-3

Television or Movie Drama Notes

Title: _____

BACKGROUND

GENRE/SUBJECT

ACTORS/ACTING

CONFLICTS

AUDIENCE APPEAL

IMPORTANT IMAGES

JOLTS

VALUES

Pembroke Publishers. © 2010 *The Writing Triangle* by Graham Foster. ISBN 978-1-55138-259-3

Problem/Solution Planning Chart

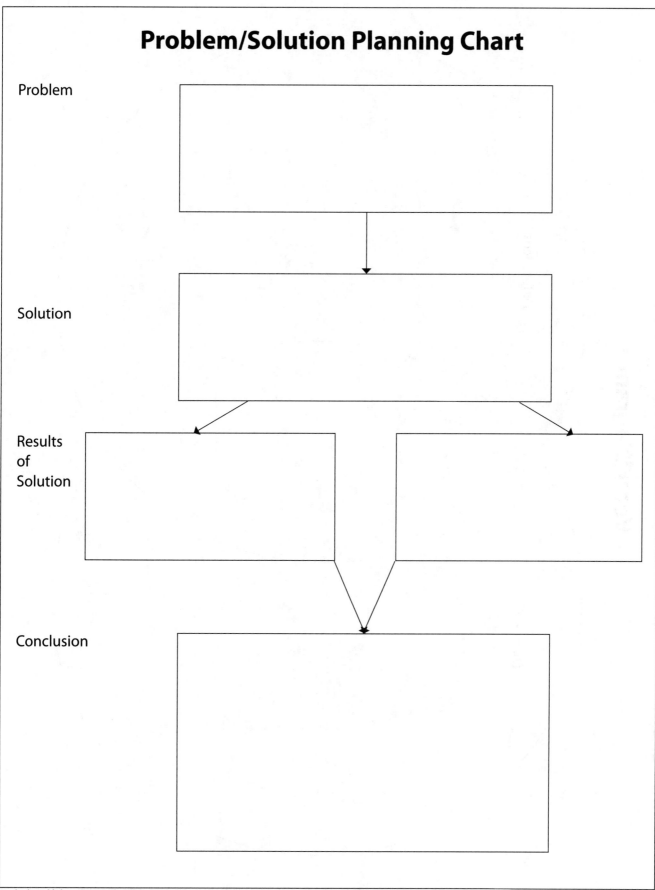

Problem

Solution

Results of Solution

Conclusion

Pembroke Publishers. © 2010 *The Writing Triangle* by Graham Foster. ISBN 978-1-55138-259-3

Venn Diagram

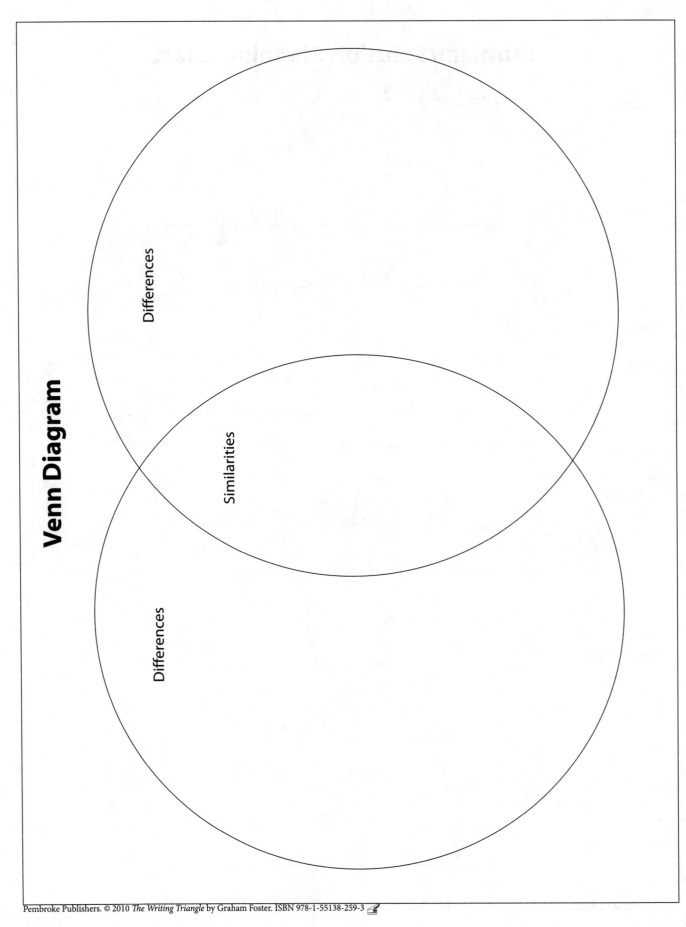

Differences

Similarities

Differences

Pembroke Publishers. © 2010 *The Writing Triangle* by Graham Foster. ISBN 978-1-55138-259-3

Comparison Frame

_____as/like _____

_____

_____

_____

_____

who/that_____

_____

_____

_____

_____

_____

_____

_____

_____

_____

_____

Index